Winning in Turbulence

Manage the Media
(Don't Let the Media Manage You)
by William J. Holstein, award-winning writer for
the *New York Times*, *Fortune*, and *Barron's*

Reward Systems: Does Yours Measure Up?
by Steve Kerr, former CLO of General Electric
and Goldman Sachs

Strategic Alliances: Three Ways to Make Them Work
by Steve Steinhilber, Vice President of Strategic
Alliances at Cisco Systems

Succession: Are You Ready?
by Marshall Goldsmith

*Top Talent: Keeping Performances Up
When Business Is Down*
by Sylvia Ann Hewlett

Winning in Turbulence

Darrell Rigby

Harvard Business Press
Boston, Massachusetts

Net Promoter® is a registered trademark of Bain & Company, Inc., Fred Reichheld, and Satmetrix Systems, Inc.

NPS℠ is a service mark of Bain & Company, Inc.

Rapid® is a registered trademark of Bain & Company, Inc.

No part of this publication may be reproduced, stored in or introduced into a retrieval system, or transmitted, in any form, or by any means (electronic, mechanical, photocopying, recording, or otherwise), without the prior permission of the publisher. Requests for permission should be directed to permissions@hbsp.harvard.edu, or mailed to Permissions, Harvard Business School Publishing, 60 Harvard Way, Boston, Massachusetts 02163.

Library of Congress Cataloging-in-Publication Data

Rigby, Darrell.
   Winning in turbulence / Darrell Rigby.
      p. cm. — (Memo to the CEO)
   ISBN 978-1-4221-3915-8 (hardcover : alk. paper) 1. Success in business.
2. Management. 3. Financial crises—History—21st century. I. Title.
   HF5386.R5123 2009
   658.4'09—dc22

                                                2009012621

The paper used in this publication meets the requirements of the American National Standard for Permanence of Paper for Publications and Documents in Libraries and Archives Z39.48-1992.

Contents

Contents

Know Where You Stand

Turbulence—a sudden change in wind speed or direction—has killed and injured more travelers than most other aviation hazards. It tests the judgment and reflexes of even the most experienced pilots. Flight crews that survive episodes of heavy turbulence talk about their disorientation and fear as the aircraft they know so well fails to respond to the controls as the ground rushes toward them.

It's a situation vividly familiar by now to many business leaders who confront an equally ominous and pervasive economic turbulence. The forces of change they grapple with are the most challenging in memory for a generation of managers. Companies are being tested to their fullest, and some will not survive.

Yet, along with the risk of disaster, turbulence also creates the opportunity to be propelled forward. The ability to navigate turbulence—to heed the warning signs and catch the updrafts—is increasingly important to success. What will separate the winners from the losers? The companies that stall or crash from those that find the updrafts?

This book is designed to provide you with the practical tools both to survive the storm and to improve your competitive position. Based on our experience working with hundreds of companies around the world, it reflects much of what we have learned from them over the years and in recent months. We hope that you will find it immediately useful, and that it helps your company not only manage effectively in turbulence but also accelerate as the economy improves.

Survival, of course, is primary and must be every company's top priority. But downturns present strategic opportunities as well as risks, with more companies recording dramatic changes than in normal times. Nearly twice as many companies moved from the top to the bottom of the pack in the 2001 recession compared with the subsequent period of economic growth, but more companies also improved their relative performance, according to a five-year study by Bain & Company that analyzed the net profit margins, sales growth, and shareholder returns of more than seven hundred and fifty companies. Although the data is not yet in on the recession that began in 2007, the fact that it has been longer, steeper, and deeper than any recession in decades suggests that the gains and losses will be even more dramatic. That's likely to mean even more turnover in the ranks of industry leaders as some companies move up and others fall back or disappear altogether.

The chapters in this book will help you end up on the right side of that ledger. They will help you clarify strategy and shift resources to core business activities. They will show how you can build flexibility in the short term by tightening cost management and improving cash flow. And they will describe practical methods of boosting revenues and margins to keep the business moving forward. Before deciding on the right tools, though, you need to know exactly where you stand.

Weathering Turbulence: Three Critical Dimensions

A tropical storm viewed from a weather satellite looks more or less uniform, as if it were affecting every area it touches with equal force. On the ground, the picture is different. One home loses its roof while others on the street come through intact. One community is devastated while its neighbor a mile away escapes unscathed.

So it is with business storms: even a sharp downturn affects everyone differently. Each company has particular strengths and vulnerabilities. Each will have different answers to three critical questions: How is the slowdown affecting the *industry* I compete in? What is my company's *strategic position* within that industry? What level of *financial resources* can my company draw on to weather the storm?

Your most powerful moves in a downturn depend on where you stand on these three dimensions. If your company has a strong financial position, for example, you may be able to out-invest competitors in marketing to increase customer loyalty. You may be able to attack or even acquire weaker competitors. If financial resources are scarce, you face a different set of possibilities. Depending on your strategic position and your industry's volatility, your best options may be to divest noncore assets and restructure the balance sheet, or to accelerate decisions around reducing cost and debt. You may need to seek alliances or merger partners and dispose of anything that is not essential to survival.

Let's look more closely at the three dimensions and at the opportunities each situation presents.

Industry Impact

Recessions hit some industries harder than others, so staying alert matters. The variations get amplified in a globalizing, interdependent economy. That adds both opportunity and complexity. The opportunity for executives is to shift a company's focus to economically healthier regions. The complexity arises from having to make long-term investments in global operations with less certainty than ever about where you will be exposed when the next downturn hits.

The United States economy provides a compelling example of the way boom and bust cycles affect industries differently. From 1987 to 2007, the United States experienced two recessions.[1] But look at what happened to specific industries in that same twenty-year period. The apparel industry weathered negative growth in thirteen out of twenty years, while the petroleum and coal industry had negative growth in ten of those years. Insurance carriers also suffered ten years of negative growth; automobile manufacturers, eight years. Real estate survived the period without any down years through 2007, but experienced massive declines in subsequent years. All are stark reminders that you're never really safe.

When recessions do hit, recovery times vary dramatically. Following the 2001 recession, the S&P 500 stock index for construction staples bounced back to positive growth in only three months, while the computer index took nine months and the telecom index almost three years to return to positive growth. Another indicator of differential impact is the gap between an industry's ten-year average growth rate and its growth during a recession year. For computers and electronics, the disparity in the 2001 recession was 25 percentage points. For broadcasting and telecommunication, the difference was only 1 point.

The current recession, too, has affected industries differently, both in the United States and around the world. Financial services firms started struggling in late 2007, especially in the United States and Europe, and entered an acute slowdown with the collapse of Lehman Brothers in September in 2008. Home construction in some countries has come to a near-standstill. Retailing activity in the United States and elsewhere declined dramatically in the fourth quarter of 2008. Most healthcare-related industries, by contrast, have continued to grow, albeit at a slower pace. One indicator of the difference: between February 2008 and February 2009 the S&P pharmaceutical index declined by 28 percent and telecommunications fell approximately 30 percent, while financials dropped by 71 percent during the same period.

Strategic Position

Within a given industry, not every company suffers equally. A company's prospects depend heavily on its strategic position.

Consider, for instance, the difference between industry leaders and followers. The returns of market leaders on average are both larger and more stable than those of followers. Many studies have borne out this relationship. *Fortune* magazine, for example, regularly compares the ten-year return of leaders in several markets with the returns of a close follower. The magazine's 2007 chart showed leaders generating total shareholder return of 267 percent over a decade, the followers only 68 percent.

Leaders are better positioned to deal with the effects of a downturn. Say that prices decline an average of 5 percent. Followers are likely to see profits turn to losses and may be forced into draconian cost-reduction programs. Leaders may record somewhat lower returns, but their profitability will usually remain above the cost of capital. They will have more flexibility to maintain or even increase spending on R&D, advertising, capacity expansion, or acquisitions.

Financial Strength

Financial resources provide the fuel for navigating through a downturn. If the fuel tank is low, the trip will be a short one. If it's full, you have options that aren't available to others. "There are enormous opportunities in recessions," Virgin Group founder

Sir Richard Branson commented in *Fortune*. "It's a good time to get brand-new planes at reasonable prices."

So you need accurate assessments of the resources available to you. What is your company's financial leverage? How much debt does it carry? What are its cash reserves? How do these numbers compare with those of your competitors? An important step for any company in a downturn is to run a series of short-term and long-term downside scenarios to determine the resources required for survival. Will you be able to refinance your debt? At what cost? Only by assessing all the potential risks can you gauge the "surplus" resources you have available for investment.

Guidelines for an Action Plan

These three dimensions—the downturn's impact on your industry, your company's strategic position, and its financial strength—can provide guidelines for an action plan calibrated to the specifics of your situation. It helps to think of a cube representing all three dimensions. By locating your company on the cube, you can focus on which actions are likely to be most effective for your situation.

Say you're in a business that is less affected even by a severe downturn. (See figure 1.) Your strategic position

FIGURE 1

Less industry sensitivity

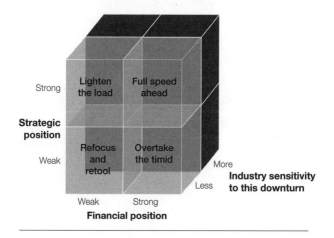

is weak but your financial position is strong, so you're in the lower right-hand quadrant of this grid, which we call "Overtake the timid." In that situation, investing in your core business is a top priority. You may want to acquire companies that can help build that core business and strengthen your strategic position. That's how LabCorp became the number-two provider of diagnostic medical testing in the United States. Taking advantage of the last downturn, it acquired three competitors in 2001 and 2002. LabCorp combined these acquisitions with its lower cost structure to underprice smaller competitors and gain additional market share.

Now flip the cube around, as we show in figure 2, and imagine that you're in an industry that has felt the effects of the downturn more acutely. If your financial and strategic positions are both strong—that is, if you're in the upper right-hand quadrant, which we call "Extend the lead"—you have some options to take advantage of competitors' weaknesses. In the last downturn, Intel Corporation effectively pulled away from Advanced Micro Devices Inc. (AMD), its scrappy rival in the chip business. Heading into the

FIGURE 2

More industry sensitivity

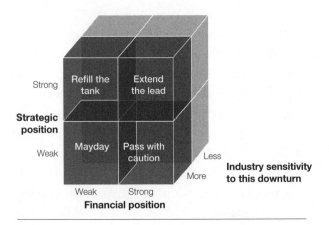

2001 recession, AMD's earlier investment in product design was paying off and its revenues were growing three times faster than Intel's. Then the recession hit, catching the entire industry with too much capacity. As AMD's lack of profitability prevented it from investing in new production facilities, Intel seized the advantage. It invested in new facilities with state-of-the-art production capability and spent heavily to advertise its P4 processors. In the ensuing years, Intel's relative cost position improved dramatically, and AMD had to slash 15 percent of its workforce. The momentum AMD had built quickly evaporated, and a reenergized Intel remained the industry leader.

Tesco, the leading retailer in the United Kingdom, was in the same position as Intel when the 2001 recession hit: strategically and financially strong. The company had missed some opportunities during the downturn of the early 1990s, but this time it was prepared. It quickly moved its advertising focus from its "Finest" line of products to "Value" products. Then it began to invest. It expanded its sales area by 10 percent annually from 2000 to 2002, triple the expansion rate of a leading competitor. It deepened its talent pool. Thanks to strategic acquisitions, it was able to roll out a new express-store format quickly. These moves enabled Tesco to avoid massive cost-reduction plans and helped it double its market-share lead over its closest rival.

Korea First Bank was in a different position—the lower right-hand corner of the cube, "Pass with caution," where companies that are strategically weak but relatively strong financially need to move with care. Driven into bankruptcy by the Asian financial crisis of the 1990s, Korea First was acquired by a foreign investment firm. Having lost its status as Korea's top corporate bank, its strategic position was weak. But thanks to the acquirer's deep pockets, its financial position was strong. Korea First used its resources to transform itself from a corporate bank into a retail bank. It shifted its branch structure to serve retail clients, built customer-service and back-office support capabilities, and remade its sales force to focus on customer service. By reducing complexity and investing selectively to focus on customers, Korea First cut loan approval time by 75 percent and reignited the bank's growth as the economy improved.

Companies in the lower left of either cube, with weak strategic and financial positions, face serious challenges. Chances are they need complete restructuring, alliances, or merger partners. They are racing time to find and sustain a viable core business. In the upper right of both quadrants the situation is reversed: companies are strong both strategically and financially. As long as they invest to protect their leadership position, they may have opportunities to gain share organically, acquire weaker competitors, or both.

As figures 1 and 2 indicate, the three dimensions of industry impact, strategic position, and financial position result in eight broad scenarios. To quickly test your company's position on these three dimensions, try answering the questions in figure 3, and then locating the cube-face quadrant that best describes your current position. For a more detailed and

---

FIGURE 3

What's Your Position?

As figures 1 and 2 indicate, the three dimensions of industry impact, strategic position, and financial position result in eight broad scenarios. To quickly test your company's position on these three dimensions, try answering the following questions, and then locating the cube-face quadrant that best describes your current position. For a more detailed and interactive diagnostic test, please visit www.harvardbusiness.org or www.bain.com/turbulence.

1 = strongly disagree, 5 = strongly agree

	1	**2**	**3**	**4**	**5**
Industry sector impact					
This downturn will shake up our industry sector—forcing capacity reductions and perhaps driving some substantial players into bankruptcy	—	—	—	—	—
This downturn will hurt sales and earnings in our industry sector harder and longer than the overall GDP	—	—	—	—	—

FIGURE 3   (continued)

	1	2	3	4	5
During this downturn, the S&P 500 will outperform our industry sector's stock price index	—	—	—	—	—
Strategic position					
Customers, vendors and other industry participants view us as one of the most admired and viable long-term competitors in our industry	—	—	—	—	—
This downturn will favor the comparative advantages (e.g., cost or quality) we have built versus key competitors	—	—	—	—	—
We have the ability to gain significant market share during this downturn, which will further enhance our ability to succeed in the upturn	—	—	—	—	—
Financial position					
Our 3-year scenarios show that we are highly confident we can meet all financial obligations and still have sufficient resources to invest in future growth opportunities	—	—	—	—	—
Our debt rating is stronger and more stable than our major competitors, who will face serious financial challenges long before we do	—	—	—	—	—
Our company is comfortable taking higher risks for potentially higher returns	—	—	—	—	—

interactive diagnostic test, please visit *www.harvard business.org* or *www.bain.com/turbulence.*

The Toolkit: An Overview

You'll need a set of specific tools to address any of these scenarios, and the key is to pick the right ones for the job. The tools you are likely to draw on reflect four broad imperatives:

- *Clarify strategy and shift resources to core business activities.* Winners in a downturn typically *invest to gain share in their core business*. The investments create or strengthen a leading position in critical market niches and give them the benefit of leadership economics. These companies also *strengthen relationships with their core customers*, building loyalty and increasing their share of wallet. Investments in *strengthening the organization* help winning companies avoid decision paralysis and focus on the decisions that matter most, then make and execute those decisions well and quickly. Some companies may opt to free up cash and management time by *divesting noncore assets*; others will choose to wait and sell those assets when market conditions improve. Either way, companies need to determine which course is right for them, and prepare assets for an effective sale.

- *Aggressively manage costs and cash flow.* Most companies can improve their performance significantly by *reducing complexity*, *streamlining back-office and other G&A functions*, and *optimizing their supply chain*. Long experience has shown that these are the most powerful cost-management levers you can pull in the short term. They'll help you gain the flexibility you need to weather a sharp downturn and invest for the future. A *receipts-and-disbursements-based cash flow tool* can help with the tight monitoring and forecasting required to ensure liquidity and meet short-term financing requirements, while *downside scenarios* that look ahead two or even three years will be important to plan effectively given the likely depth and scope of this downturn.

- *Increase revenue and margins.* Is your salesforce as productive as it could be? Many companies have shored up declining sales and even increased revenue quickly by *restructuring and refocusing their sales reps*. A series of data-driven tools help reps concentrate on the right targets, manage their pipeline effectively, and maximize customer face time—all essential in the current market. To maintain margin, you need to *price for margin or share gains*. Pricing has a greater effect on profits than any other managerial tool, yet pricing capabilities remain underdeveloped at many companies.

- *Prepare for bold moves.* Because so many companies are struggling, a downturn brings the possibility of *game-changing acquisitions and partnerships*. If you have a strong financial position, you can make use of the downturn to consolidate or expand your market position and acquire capabilities at bargain prices. Even companies that were once unapproachable may welcome partnerships they spurned in better times.

Each of these tools will be described in more detail in the following chapters. Some tools will be more relevant and effective than others, depending on your company's situation (figure 4). As you read the chapters, you can check to see whether each tool described is practical and effective for your company.

The current turbulence presents companies with major long-term challenges. Some firms won't rise to the occasion. They'll fall back in the pack, be acquired, or face bankruptcy. But downturns create opportunities as well as risks. With a practical action plan that reflects a firm's unique position and puts the right tools to work immediately, companies can emerge from the storm stronger than ever.

FIGURE 4

Winning in this downturn: Pull the right levers for your situation

Legend:
- ● Most critical levers
- ○ Secondary priorities
- ⬤ Combine with winners

	Industry sensitivity	Less				More			
	Strategic position	Strong	Strong	Weak	Weak	Strong	Strong	Weak	Weak
	Financial position	Strong	Weak	Strong	Weak	Strong	Weak	Strong	Weak
		Full speed ahead	Lighten the load	Overtake the timid	Refocus & retool	Extend the lead	Refill the tank	Pass with caution	Mayday
Clarify strategies and shift resources to core activities									
1	Business strategy—choose where and how to win	●	●	●		●		●	
2	Customer strategy—protect and grow customer loyalty	●	●	●	○	●		●	
3	Organization strategy—strengthen the organization			○		●		●	
Aggressively manage costs and cash flow									
4	Manage complexity to drive performance improvement	○	●	●	●	●	●	●	●
5	Streamline G&A	○	●	●	●	●	●	●	●
6	Tightly manage cash flows and liquidity			○	●	●	●	●	●
Increase revenues and margins									
7	Turbocharge sales	●	○	○	○	●		○	
8	Price for today and tomorrow	●	○	○		●		○	
Prepare for bold moves									
9	Pursue game-changing acquisitions and partnerships	●		●	⬤	●	○	○	⬤

Testing Your Firm's Readiness

To perform effectively in a downturn, you need an action plan grounded in your company's specific situation and the right management tools to carry it out. You also need a strong set of core values that consistently guides the necessary trade-offs. To test your firm's readiness, try asking your management team the four questions below:

What are our objectives, priorities, and values? A turbulent environment forces leaders to know what they value most and act accordingly. Is revenue growth more important than cost reduction? Is market share more valuable than profit margins? How important is the continuing loyalty of employees and customers—as compared, for example, with hitting quarterly earnings targets?

What are the most important decisions we will make? Long before making a decision, the best companies discuss what will need to be decided. Research shows that executives under stress typically reach for the same levers they have pulled in the past. It's better to make sure you're reaching for the right levers before you start pulling anything at all.

What changing conditions could we encounter? Today's downturn is testing companies and their executive teams as they have rarely been tested before, and nobody has a crystal ball. As you plan, make a point of encouraging "company Cassandras"—people who will generate plausible worst-case scenarios. These scenarios will help you understand what will be required for survival.

What conditions would trigger a change in course? Every company needs a well-grounded understanding of when to begin implementing its contingency plans.

Decide right now what environmental and marketplace changes you will monitor. Then determine what level of change in either direction would dictate a shift to "Plan B" (further measures to protect your strategic position and profitability) or "Plan A+" (moves to help you accelerate out of the downturn).

These questions are only a start. Most executives and leadership teams are grappling with these issues in one form or another. That sets them on a path to survive in turbulence and accelerate when the economy starts to improve.

Clarify Strategy

Choose Where and How to Win

When a person's life is threatened, the body adapts superbly for fight or flight. Blood flow is diverted to the lungs and other critical areas. The pupils dilate to improve vision, and hearing is sharper. Breathing, heart rates, and response times accelerate. The odds of survival improve.

If only a company could respond so brilliantly to the dangers of a downturn. Instead, executives often struggle to distinguish between core activities and less vital functions. They look inward rather than outward. Their decisions are hampered by loss of concentration, diminished creativity, and an inability to perceive and learn from new information. When that happens, the odds of survival deteriorate.

The goal of strategy in a downturn is to help you end up on the right side of the mortality tables—not just surviving but poised for growth, as Darwinian forces eliminate weaker competitors. To build that strategy, you need to know exactly where you will compete, how you plan to win, and how you will mobilize the organization to implement the strategy.

Where to Compete: Defining the Core

In good times, companies expand their operations. They add product lines, expand into new geographic areas and customer segments, and even experiment with new business models. Then comes a downturn. The company can no longer do everything it once did, and the decisions about where to focus can be agonizing. Traditional strongholds may be profitable, but can they deliver sufficient growth? New business arenas are growing, but they are proving far more challenging than expected. Besides, we launched them with such fanfare—won't we look ridiculous if we cut them back so soon?

Bain's analysis shows that concentrating on a company's core business dramatically improves the odds of success in a downturn. About 95 percent of the companies that we call sustained value creators—those that maintained at least a 5.5 percent real growth rate in revenue and profit over ten years while earning back their cost of capital—are leaders in their core businesses. Strong cores also helped this group perform better and recover faster in the last downturn: average net profit margins bounced back to 6.5 percent in 2002, only slightly below pre-recession levels in 2000. Their competitors fared much worse, with average net profit margins falling to around 1 percent during the same period, a drop of about 3 percentage points. Again, it's like the human body: faced with threats, it relies on the fundamental systems at its core that afford the best chance of survival.

But deciding to focus on the core is much easier than finding it and developing its full potential.

Defining the core begins with an outside-in view: delineating the markets you operate in, assessing what is happening in those markets, and defining the company's strategic position in each one. How are customers' needs changing? Where might competitors be newly vulnerable? This is not an exercise in listening for what you want to hear, with conclusions that flatter your accomplishments; it's based on a robust definition of the boundaries between markets and a realistic assessment of competitive position. And it's a critically important step in a downturn, because the wrong market definition can lead to strategic missteps even when times are good. In the late 1990s, for example, Gillette decided to view its core business as "checkout purchases" and thus diversified into batteries and writing instruments. But these businesses had little in common with Gillette's razor business, so synergies were few. The company struggled, and its stock price fell by more than 60 percent between 1998 and 2001.

The outside-in view, in turn, sets the context for a thorough inside-out analysis. Where is the company generating the best results, measured by profitability and growth? Which product lines, which markets, which customer segments? With this fundamental data in hand, you can ask two critical questions that managers often miss.

- *Who are the customers that we love the most—and that love us the most?* Imagine a grid showing the profitability of different customer segments on one axis and the loyalty of customers in those segments on the other. In the upper right-hand corner are the customers who generate the most profits, and who can scarcely get enough of what you offer them. They are your "profitable promoters"—the ones who will buy from you repeatedly, sing your praises to their friends, and make money for you. They are at the heart of your business.

- *What unique advantages do we have?* A company's unique capabilities can be as important as its best customers. It may have exceptional engineering skills, like Intel, or marketing abilities, like Nike. It may have created a distinctive set of relationships with customers. Singapore-based Olam International, a leader in the business of supplying agricultural commodities from emerging markets to large food processors in the developed world, got its start by developing exceptional skills in managing the price and foreign-currency risks that are endemic to the business. Companies may also have a distinctive set of assets, such as De Beers's diamond mines or Disney's cartoon characters, or a dominant share of particular markets. All these can give them an economic advantage that no one else has, at least for a while.

Such advantages help companies decide where to compete, and in a downturn they're more important than ever. Procter & Gamble, for instance, has always owned a strong set of brands with loyal customers in many segments. In recent years it has reinforced those all-important customer relationships through continuous innovation designed to deliver specific benefits to customers. As a result, P&G can compete effectively—and retain more of its customers—in any area where it decides to focus these capabilities.

How to Win: The Repeatable, Adaptable Model

How do you know if your core business can compete successfully? Short-term financial measures don't always provide reliable insights into the health of a core or what may be required for it to succeed. There is simply too much noise in the signal—too many variables that affect performance—to have confidence in the message. A 20 percent drop in revenue, for instance, may reflect the immediate impact of a downturn or it may signify a troubled core.

Repeatability

The key to a strong core business is a *repeatable formula* that allows the company to reinforce and expand the core in ways that won't later require retrenchment. The formula defines how the company intends to win. Its repeatability conditions the organization to move quickly and instinctively, the way years of practice help great athletes develop the muscle memory that enables them to compete at the highest levels.

Compare the histories of Nike and Reebok, for example. In 1987 Nike's operating profits were $164 million to Reebok's $309 million, and Nike's market valuation was half that of Reebok's. Fifteen years (and two downturns) later the situation was reversed: now

Nike's profits were $1.1 billion while Reebok's had declined to $247 million. The difference was that Nike had developed the repeatable model that enabled it to expand its core business systematically from jogging to volleyball to tennis to basketball to soccer and so on. Nike executives told us that this model was built on four core capabilities that remained constant throughout the company's history: world-class brand management, an ability to develop sports stars as brand icons, superior R&D capabilities in shoes, and a strong apparel supply chain. Reebok, meanwhile, veered from one business to the next with no clear plan. Unrelated investments such as the acquisition of the Boston Whaler boat company sapped the company's strength just as its core shoe business came under attack.

In our experience, most successful strategies are based on some kind of repeatable model that strengthens and expands the core. The power of a repeatable model is its simplicity. Everyone in the organization, in effect, knows the business's priorities, and has the skills and capabilities to make the core as strong as it can be. They can move fast when opportunities arise. In a slow economy, all that is invaluable.

Adaptability

Repeatable, however, doesn't mean *unchanging*. In fact, Darwin would say that adaptability is at least as important as fitness for survival, and recessions have a way of accelerating Darwinian shakeouts. The reason, of course, is that nothing holds steady in a downturn. Companies must make tough choices about which markets they can compete in most effectively and then revisit those choices as new information becomes available. They must make hard decisions about where they will develop world-class capabilities and assets and where they will be satisfied with "good enough" for now. Those decisions, too, need to be revisited regularly.

To react quickly and effectively to what's happening in their markets and industries, companies need a system for gathering and acting on feedback from the front lines of the business. The human body constantly scans the environment for changes in temperature, food supply, competitive threats, and other vital factors. Changes in the environment trigger immediate adaptations in metabolic rates, adrenaline levels, even perspiration. Companies can learn to do the same. For example, they can do a quick "Net Promoter® Score (NPS)" survey of customers after every transaction, asking how likely it is that the customers would recommend the company or the product to a friend or colleague. Answers to this question—scored on a zero-to-10 scale—correlate highly with customer loyalty and can serve as an early warning of incipient dissatisfaction or defection. The brokerage firm Charles Schwab, for example, used the Net Promoter system to reverse declines in revenue and profits and recover its market position. Schwab cut its prices to re-establish its position as a value leader. It also eliminated "nuisance" fees and invested in service improvements at every level. Schwab constantly monitored its NPS^{SM} survey scores during these moves, using the client feedback loops to keep the organization focused on clients and make sure its new strategy was on the right track. We cover NPS in more detail in chapter 3.

Rigorous feedback loops are invaluable in a downturn, as companies try to determine whether customer priorities are changing and whether the specific economic advantages of their repeatable model continues to apply. The U.K. retailer Tesco's repeatable model is its ability to open store after store and to cater effectively to different customer segments with different store formats. As the current recession took hold in the United Kingdom, Tesco saw that its customers were looking for value-priced products, and so began emphasizing value rather than premium lines.

Often, the keys to adapting a company's repeatable model are found within the company's existing business. Unilever, for instance, has responded to recessionary trends in the United States and Europe by expanding an innovative rural distribution model led by women's self-help groups to several emerging markets. Hindustan Unilever's *Shakti* program, which enables unemployed rural women in India to set themselves up in business as direct-to-home distributors of Unilever's consumer products, is being adapted to Sri Lanka, Vietnam, and Bangladesh. The women sell the products—usually in small, inexpensive packages—in rural villages not reached by other distribution channels. Unilever aims to use the low-cost distribution network to tap fresh avenues of growth in Asian, African, and Latin American markets.

Strengthening the Core

Companies with a formula built into the organization's muscle memory can often invest to strengthen it, even during a slowdown. They naturally tailor investment levels to the economic climate and available financial resources, and they emphasize adaptability as well as repeatability. But they don't let up, and that steady persistence helps them pull away from competitors. Southwest Airlines is a prime example. During the 2001–2002 downturn it discounted fares heavily, boosting demand and reinforcing its positioning as the leading low-fare airline. It invested only modestly in capacity growth, less than it might have in normal times but still enough to hone its repeatable model of expanding into new regional markets. It also launched an aggressive advertising campaign to build its base of loyal customers. Thanks to these moves, Southwest emerged from the downturn with greater market share.

Sometimes the best way to strengthen the core is to refocus it, selling off businesses that are less closely related so the company can grow around a more tightly defined core. General Dynamics pursued this strategy in the early 1990s. Facing a prolonged slowdown in the defense industry, General Dynamics began divesting companies in aerospace and missile systems, where it had no chance of establishing leadership. Revenue declined, but profitability increased. The company then began reinvesting in a better-defined core, bolstering its marine systems business through acquisitions and building a new, related core in electronics and defense information systems. By 2005 its revenue and profit growth marked it as the best-performing defense company in the United States during this period.

How to Mobilize: The Change Model

In a downturn a company must respond quickly to threats. The strategy often shifts from expansion to reinforcing the core. Changes like these can be unsettling to people in an organization—one reason for the slowness and confusion that often characterize companies' responses to a recession. The challenge is to help people understand the new direction and enable them to work in concert rather than at cross purposes. We call this *mobilization*, and it's an essential part of a strategy designed to strengthen the core.

Mobilization spells out the *what*, *who*, and *when* of change, but it particularly focuses on the *why* and the *how*. Both are essential in a recession. Understanding the reasons for change is critical, because people must believe they will emerge from the turbulence as winners. If they believe they are relying on a bad business model, they won't engage. The *how* of change is equally important. Companies habitually expect more of their employees in a recession, often because they have reduced head count. But you can't engage people by asking them to do the same things at, say, 20 percent less cost. They need to believe that what they are doing now—implementing the new strategy—will lead to a better future.

Mobilization starts early, as soon as the strategy itself is being determined. In the first phase of a change effort, managers naturally focus on assembling the fact base and creating alternatives. But companies preparing for mobilization will already be assessing the challenge of rallying the entire organization behind the strategy. In the second phase, most attention focuses on making strategic choices; companies should also weigh the practical requirements of implementing each option. The third phase then focuses on mobilization itself. Change leaders must create a compelling vision and communicate it all the way through to the front line. They must define clear roles for implementing the change and launch the right initiatives to get it started. They must set up effective project management capabilities, complete with contingency plans and well-defined accountabilities.

A downturn tests the core. When you mobilize to strengthen it, you find out how strong your repeatable model is, and how adaptable. It's a moment of truth, and a vital measure of your company's ability to fight in segments where it has decided to compete, flee other segments, and emerge from the trauma stronger than before.

Protect and Grow Customer Loyalty

Economic downturns wreak havoc with customer relationships. Deep cost-cutting compromises service. Layoffs and pay freezes leave front-line employees demoralized. To make up for lost revenues, companies sometimes look for ways to tack on new charges and fees, which make customers feel they are being gouged.

Some companies tolerate this abuse of customers as unfortunate collateral damage in a recession. After all, aren't competitors exploiting customers, too? But the negative effects of lost customer trust can be deep and long-lasting. And the advantages of loyalty are even more pronounced in a downturn. Loyal customers cost less to serve. They typically concentrate more of their spending with companies they trust to meet their needs and treat them well. They are less likely to defect than shoppers whose attachment to a company is no deeper than the latest price discount.

Loyal customers also help stretch marketing dollars. Their word-of-mouth referrals to friends and associates provide a company with more like-minded customers, laying the foundation for growth when the economy turns around.

The powerful advantages of customer loyalty help explain why the biggest changes in market share occur during downturns. Many companies do well when consumer spending rises and the economy is expanding. But when spending drops, the companies focused on protecting and growing their most loyal, profitable customer segments often manage to stabilize their business. They may even attract new customers as competitors falter. Until the equity markets began to slide in 2008, for example, mutual fund companies of nearly all stripes prospered. Many investors chased hot returns, and many fund companies were happy to oblige them with an array of trendy offerings. But as returns dropped, customers quickly sold their shares. That didn't happen at Vanguard. The pioneer of market index investing remained focused on keeping costs low, offering funds with clear, easy-to-understand investment strategies, and maintaining great service. That approach has once again enabled Vanguard to outperform competitors during the current recession: in 2008, Vanguard enjoyed net cash inflows of $71 billion compared with net outflows of $225 billion for the rest of the industry, according to the Investment Company Institute. And Vanguard continues to gain market share, as it has done through market downturns over more than twenty-five years.

But maintaining customer loyalty in a downturn is a difficult challenge. Nearly all customers, including the most loyal, are more sensitive to price than before. Aggressive rivals may try to lure them with discounts and rebates. If you aren't the low-cost provider in your industry, you may not be able to match those price cuts. And as we'll explain, that may not be the best strategy in any case. Most people buy on value, not price alone. But the situation does require new strategic thinking. How have your customers' preferences changed? How long will those changes last? How can you appeal to their new needs without diluting your long-term competitive advantage?

In our experience, the companies that answer those questions effectively and strengthen loyalty in a downturn share some common characteristics:

- They steer clear of three specific traps. If one of them snares you, you won't get the chance to do anything else.

- They avoid confusion about their customer "sweet spot"—the customers who matter most to the success of their business—and selectively add segments that extend and reinforce the target without diluting the brand or adding costly complexity.

- They ensure that those customers have the best possible experiences where it counts the most.

Let's take a look at how loyalty leaders follow a common course in a downturn.

Avoiding the Traps

Trap number one is chasing revenues by trying to appeal to every potential customer group, often through aggressive discounting. These moves can seem logical and urgent in a downturn. Customers buy less, yet industry capacity is slow to adjust. Rivals compete aggressively for marginal sales. The trouble is, not all incremental sales are equal. The new customers attracted only by lower prices often fail to buy more when prices recover. Moreover, they sometimes place additional demands on the business system, creating unexpected new costs.

Saks Fifth Avenue encountered this trap during the 2001 recession, implementing deep price cuts that temporarily boosted revenues but undercut its luxury status for many longtime customers. Nieman Marcus assumed the luxury mantle, and when the economy rebounded, Saks's sales were slower to recover. In the brutal retail environment of the current recession, Saks has followed a similar course, abruptly cutting prices of designer clothes by 70 percent in November 2008. Though the deep discounts provoked a rush of shoppers, Saks risked losing still more ground with the luxury-goods consumers who were once its core customers.

Trap number two is indiscriminate cost cutting. The most effective companies acknowledge that downturns require painful reductions in product and service offerings to offset declining margins. But they cut costs with a scalpel rather than a meat ax, paying close attention to their most important customers. Under pressure to prune the number of products it stocked in a weakening economy, for example, one supermarket chain reduced costs by weeding out all the items that failed to generate a threshold level of returns. But store revenues continued to fall far below expectations. When the company probed deeper, it discovered that three of the items it had cut—an artisanal cheese, specialty bread, and a tropical fruit—were especially popular with a significant number of its top-spending loyal customers. No longer finding the goods they prized on store shelves, they began to shop elsewhere. A quick round of market research indicated that these customers were actually willing to pay more for the special products they liked. When the items were reinstated, higher-spending customers gradually trickled back in to the stores.

Trap number three is reducing investment in customer-focused innovation. There's no evidence that new-product introductions tail off in downturns, so you can't assume your competitors are cutting back on this front. Breakthrough products and services like the iPod, Xbox, Zipcar, JetBlue's low-cost flights, and the Kindle 2 e-book reader were all introduced during recessions, attracting new customers while competitors struggled. The most effective companies stay focused on the capabilities they'll need to serve their most important customers in two or three years. They use the crisis of a downturn to rally the organization around the innovations that deliver a better customer experience, both now and in the future.

Find Your Customer Sweet Spot

Simply avoiding the traps isn't enough, of course. A company also has to maintain a strong external focus and apply a set of practical disciplines that keep its most important customers front and center. That's harder than it seems. In a downturn every company faces difficult choices about which customers it will fight to keep and which it will pass up. That requires the right information and insights to answer some key strategic questions: What customer segments are out there and how differentiated are they? How capable are you of actually meeting different segments' needs? Can you do so without diluting what you offer your most important customers? Segmentation strategies often fail during downturns because marketers cast their nets too wide, in an attempt to capture large, amorphous customer groups. By trying to satisfy all these groups, companies end up creating watered-down offerings that fail to excite anyone.

To make the right trade-offs, management teams first need to identify an attractive customer core that becomes the prime focus of their energies and investments. We call this group the *design target*. The design target comprises the heart of the segment to which your company sells. It's the group that your company comes to understand so completely that when you design products and services for them, they say: this is absolutely perfect for me. They're the customers your company can serve better than any competitor can. By doing so, you will attract others who are like them.

These customers tend to have three vital traits. They are disproportionately valuable in the amount of business they do with you now and in their potential worth to your company over the long term.

They are highly loyal; they stick with your company through good times and bad. Finally, they are especially influential in the marketplace; their tastes and preferences influence or lead large populations who may want your company's products and services and whom you will want to reach. So even though the design target itself may be small, it is representative of a broad range of customers. BMW, for example, designs its cars for the relatively small group of people who truly treasure high performance and immaculate attention to detail, all for a reasonable price. One of the defining characteristics of this group, which BMW calls the "active affluent," is how they describe the elation they feel when accelerating a great car around a curve. Yet the company's products appeal to a broad range of buyers who may never make full use of the engine's power or the suspension's precise road handling.

Large companies, of course, appeal to multiple customer segments, which may mean identifying more than one design target. The buyer of BMW's Mini Cooper is different from the buyer of its M3 convertible. The issue then is how the company can meet the needs of different segments without diluting its brand image among core customers and without adding too much cost or complexity. Some companies elect to serve different segments through separate brands, channels, or both. Others tailor their products, services, and marketing strategies to appeal to different segments. But that's the value of the design target: those customers will let you know if you risk alienating them. If you do, watch out.

Promoters, Passives, and Detractors

A simple way to find this elite inner circle is first to identify discrete customer segments based on their different needs, attitudes, and behaviors. Next, sort your current customers in each segment by profitability and potential value. Then group them into "promoters," "passives," or "detractors" by asking them to rate on a scale of zero to 10: *How likely are you to recommend our company's products or services to a friend or a colleague?* Those responding with scores of 9 or 10 are promoters, your company's biggest boosters. Those answering with a 7 or 8 are passives, lukewarm at best to your company. Those giving a score of 6 or less are detractors. This group is dissatisfied with your company and is apt to drive away potential new customers through negative word-of-mouth. Subtracting the percentage of detractors from the percentage of promoters yields a company's Net Promoter Score (NPS), which measures the degree of loyalty among a company's customers.

One way to think about this is to visualize a grid that lays out each customer segment in a scatter plot, with their loyalty to your company on the x-axis and their profitability on the y-axis. Customers in the upper right-hand corner—profitable promoters with homogeneous needs, attitudes and behaviors—form the heart of your potential design target. This group appreciates what you are providing them today and their profitability makes them important to your business during the downturn and beyond.

Defining the right core customer segment to pursue is the starting point of a virtuous cycle for boosting profitability and market share. Coming out of the 2001 downturn, for example, Vodafone Group, the U.K.–based wireless telecom services provider, used a similar approach to identify five high-potential customer segments in its design target. Homing in on the combinations of convenience, value, and lifestyle that best met these customers' needs, the company developed new service plans to reach each one. By attaching a face, voice, and wallet to each sharply etched core customer, Vodafone scored significant market share gains in eight of the ten markets in which it competed.

Concrete metrics like Net Promoter Score help sharpen a company's focus on loyal customers based on what they say and do. The metrics help to identify what loyal customers like most about today's products and services—important to maintain at all costs—as well as actions that drive core customers away. Loyalty leaders use this understanding to probe deeper into the behaviors as well as the emotions of these consumers. Many customers, after all, say they love a particular product or service until something dramatically new and different shows up in the marketplace. Anticipating breakthrough changes means moving beyond quantitative research; it means studying customers closely and trying to figure out what they truly value most. Intuit, for example, makes detailed observations of selected customers as they begin to use the company's financial software. LEGO works closely with online and offline communities of fans to guide new product development and pricing decisions. Although it takes resources to stay attuned to consumers' unformed wants and needs, these investments pay off for companies trying to find new ways to appeal to customers in a downturn and when the economy improves.

Invest in "Moments of Truth"

Customer loyalty is earned one transaction at a time. From the handling of an initial sale to the attentiveness of call-center personnel to the management of contract renewals, each customer contact is an opportunity to win a promoter, convert a passive customer into a fan, or disarm a detractor. During a downturn, those interactions take on added importance as customers seek more value for each dollar they spend. But not all customer experiences are equally important. That's why customer-focused companies take pains to identify the critical moments of truth that have the greatest potential to delight customers—or to drive them away.

One way to determine which touchpoints matter most is to ask customers directly. Contact them two or three weeks after a purchase, a warranty repair or other direct interactions with your organization's front line. Invite them to rate how likely they would be to recommend the company based on that most recent experience, and give them an opportunity to explain why they gave that rating. Then feed that information back to the front line. Follow up with respondents who agree to be contacted by calling them, enabling front-line employees to uncover the root causes of problems that annoy customers and make quick, continuous adjustments. The follow-up calls also help front-line employees understand what they did to create promoters—a reward that is easily overlooked but can inject an important boost to morale during a downturn.

Closing the feedback loop in this way can provide a cost-effective early warning system for identifying service gaps before they become major issues. By continuously analyzing customer feedback about its claims settlement procedures, for example, auto insurer Progressive Corp., learned how sensitive policyholders were to reimbursement delays when their vehicles had been damaged beyond repair. Like most insurers, Progressive organized its claims processing for internal efficiency. But when operations managers dug into the customer survey results, they discovered that their NPS dropped precipitously with customers who had to wait too long for reimbursement. By fine-tuning how claims were routed, Progressive shortened the payment cycle from initial filing to the customer's receipt of a check by more than 35 percent and saw its NPS jump by more than 50 percentage points.

Getting Started

Progressive Corp. and other loyalty leaders have distinct advantages during a downturn. But companies that didn't invest in building loyalty before the crisis hit can still make substantial gains quickly by taking some practical steps. You can begin by identifying your most loyal and profitable customers, understanding what they most like about you, and determining what you can do to improve their experience. Who among these customers are we failing to satisfy fully? What must we do to root out business processes that aggravate those customers? You may find that you can strengthen relationships with your most important customers while also reducing costs. For example, American Express found millions of dollars in savings in less than a year through quick process fixes that resulted in fewer service calls, fewer complaints, fewer follow-up calls, and less need for rework.

At a time when companies are seeking every possible advantage they can wield in a tough economy, keeping loyal customers front and center can make a critical difference—both now and in the long term.

Strengthen the Organization

Who's got time to worry about building a stronger organization in an acute downturn? Surely executives can't focus on internal issues when so many other pressing matters are crowding in on them.

In fact, this is exactly the time when leaders need to ensure their organizations are performing well, so that important decisions get made and executed quickly and effectively. Turbulence creates exceptional opportunities for some organizations and extraordinary urgency for others. None should be satisfied with the status quo.

It's clear enough how a company that is relatively strong can gain by strengthening its organization. Turbulence offers a rare chance to bring in new talent and improve the way that organizations function. But while skepticism from executives under stress is natural, companies in dire straits have everything to gain from investing in their organizations. They often lack the organizational capabilities to take on the challenges they face. Some rush to snap judgments and ill-considered decisions. Others stall, unable to make key decisions. Some of these companies badly need new people and the perspectives they bring to help the business survive. They may need to overhaul dysfunctional cultures—the kind, for instance, that supported excessive risk and reward without accountability. They certainly need to revisit the questionable decision processes that landed them in so much trouble.

The fact is, strengthening the organization is one of the most powerful levers any company can pull to improve its performance in a downturn. As we say throughout this book, industries are affected differently by different recessions. Individual companies occupy stronger or weaker competitive positions. Some have adequate financial resources; others are strapped for cash. These differences determine a company's action plan in turbulence.

But even though the situations and necessary actions vary widely, the questions that companies must ask to strengthen their organizations are largely the same. What are the critical decisions we must address in this downturn? Do we need to adjust our organizational structure to address them effectively? How should our roles and processes change? Will our most experienced people be able to make and execute the key decisions, or are new skills and perspectives required? Which aspects of our culture reinforce decision effectiveness, and which should be thrown out?

Adopting this "decision lens"—by identifying the critical decisions and then determining what needs to change in order to help the organization make and execute those decisions effectively—is the single most important step a company can take to improve the performance of its organization. It helps leaders focus their efforts where they will have the most impact during a downturn. And it positions the company to accelerate when the economy turns around.

Identifying the Critical Decisions

Every company has its own set of critical decisions. If your business is in relatively good shape, those decisions may not have changed much. Some will be the big choices made by the senior team and the board, such as whether to acquire a competitor or invest in a new product. Others may be decisions made every day on the front line. Toyota, for example, achieved its leading position partly through its reputation for top-of-the-line manufacturing quality. To maintain that quality, Toyota had to ensure that workers in every plant (and in suppliers' plants) knew how to make and execute the right quality-related decisions during the production process. These decisions are no less important now than when Toyota was growing rapidly.

If you're in survival mode, the list of critical decisions will be different. The most important decisions bear on your ability to stay in business, like whether to sell a stake in the company or overhaul the business model. Everyday decisions relating to cost reduction, cash management, and pricing take on critical importance. So do some of the key decisions made in the past—decisions that may have been right at the time but are now hurting the business. A once-promising acquisition may need to be sold. Compensation systems may need to be revamped and major contracts renegotiated. When survival is at stake, no company can take past decisions for granted.

Once you've identified your critical decisions, you need effective systems for making and executing them. Strong companies make sure that their structure isn't getting in the way. They define clear decision roles and ensure that people with the necessary skills and capabilities are in the roles where they can have the greatest impact.

Testing the Structure

Downturns force many companies to restructure their organizations, by centralizing decision making, for example, or consolidating divisions. Structural change can be distracting and cause upheaval at a time when companies need to be externally focused, so there should be a high bar for such changes. But sometimes structure is a serious obstacle to making and executing a business's critical decisions. In that case, structure has to change.

At Hewlett-Packard, for example, the company's salesforce used to be organized by customer while its manufacturing units were organized by product. It was a classic structural bottleneck: decisions stalled, people worked at cross-purposes, and HP's performance suffered. The company's leaders responded by shifting to a product-based structure across the entire company, with accountabilities for decisions clearly defined. That created the conditions for better decision making and execution, which in turn generated higher profitability.

A downturn can magnify the need for this kind of structural change. Companies may need to improve accountability and break through decision bottlenecks. Financial pressures can also be a catalyst for adjusting a company's detailed structure. For example, many companies take this opportunity to simplify their organizations, adjusting management layers and spans of control with the goal of increasing both efficiency and effectiveness. Under pressure to improve performance,

Intel restructured in 2006, removing two layers of the organization and increasing the span of control for each manager by two or three people. The resulting decrease in cost and complexity was one important factor contributing to improved operating income: Intel's operating income rose 45 percent between 2006 and 2007.

Clarifying Roles and Processes

Whatever a company's structure, decision roles need to be clear and unambiguous. Unless people know who's responsible for making and executing critical decisions, the stress on the organization will only increase. A tool we call RAPID® clarifies accountabilities for each part of these decisions.

RAPID is a loose acronym for the key roles in any major decision. The individual or team responsible for a *recommendation* gathers relevant information and comes up with a proposed course of action. People with *input* responsibilities are consulted about the recommendation. They help shape a recommendation so that it is operationally practical, financially feasible, and so on. An executive who must *agree* is anyone who needs to sign off on the proposal—often a legal or regulatory compliance officer.

Eventually, one person will *decide*. We say that person "has the D." The decision maker needs good business judgment, a grasp of the relevant trade-offs, and a keen awareness of the organization that will execute the decision. Assigning the D to one individual ensures single-point accountability. The final role in the process involves the people who will *perform* or execute the decision. This is a crucial role to assign, since people with "P" responsibility are not always involved in making the decision.

Clear decision roles are essential in turbulent times: they can boost performance by unclogging bottlenecks and cutting the organization's cycle time. In the last downturn, for instance, the European division of a U.S. telecommunications company was always behind its competitors in submitting bids to customers. The reason: every bid had to be routed through U.S. headquarters for approval. A RAPID analysis helped U.S. executives see that European sales managers could have the D for submissions, enabling the organization to operate faster. In our experience, companies that implement RAPIDs start to use a powerful new vocabulary that reinforces the new way of thinking about decisions. ("Who has the D here?") That, too, helps the organization work faster and more effectively.

For clear decision roles to have their full impact, they must be supported by rigorous decision processes. The people participating in a decision need to be involved at the right time, gather all the facts necessary to evaluate alternatives against well-defined criteria, and commit the resources to follow through.

Putting the Right People in the Right Roles

When times are good, companies tend to focus on how to manage their growing organizations. In a downturn, the logic changes. Companies have to cut costs. Many do so by letting people go, difficult though it may be. But layoffs and attrition create problems of their own. The people who leave are not always the poorest performers. Those who stay may not have the skills and capabilities to make and execute the decisions required by the current environment. And because companies are in cost-reduction mode, they often fail to consider who they might *hire* to bolster their capabilities. Ultimately, individuals must make and execute every critical decision. And no company in a recession can afford to have the wrong people in key decision roles.

Here, too, a downturn is an opportunity to improve the caliber of the organization. Veteran managers, for instance, are sometimes prisoners of their experience and unable to cope with the requirements of a new situation. People coming in from other companies or even other industries can shed new light on strategic and operational challenges. Even without new blood from the outside, companies often can strengthen an organization by moving people to roles where they have the most impact. At one technology company, we found that more than 40 percent of managers identified as high performers were in positions deemed non-critical. Meanwhile, fewer than 40 percent of the company's mission-critical roles were occupied by top performers. The senior team acted quickly to correct the mismatch, and the performance of the business started to improve immediately.

The key to making the best possible use of people is a robust, effective performance-management system. Most companies already have the elements of performance management in place, and some parts of the process may be first-rate. But many suffer from problems such as grade inflation. One mining company, for instance, rated fully 80 percent of its people as above average, even though the company had been underperforming for years. The system also needs to carry real consequences. If differences in evaluation actually lead to differences in outcomes such as career opportunities, mentoring and coaching, compensation, retention efforts, then line managers (and everyone else) will take the evaluations seriously. At the mining company, senior executives tightened up the rating process and made the consequences of ratings more explicit. High performers received increases in pay along with better career development and training opportunities and better retention packages. Those with lower ratings received coaching and eventual outplacement if necessary. The system finally had teeth—and leaders throughout the organization could accurately gauge the quality of the people available and put their top talent in positions that mattered most to the success of the business.

Actively Managing the Culture

Culture underpins the decisions an organization makes and executes. It defines "the way we do things around here." As one observer said, it determines how people act when no one is looking. But cultures can change over time and are particularly susceptible to change when the organization is in crisis. In an acute downturn, leaders need to take deliberate action to keep a strong culture from deteriorating—or to transform a culture that gets in the way of good decisions.

Understanding that its culture is a competitive advantage, Southwest Airlines reinforces it in hard times. The airline is committed to the highest quality of customer service and to providing employees with a stable working environment. In the early stages of the

2007 recession, Southwest made decisions consistent with these principles, maintaining staff loyalty—in part through no involuntary job cuts—and investing in upgrading its customer service. The carrier continues to be a leader in on-time performance, an aspect of the business that matters a lot to customers.

No company can avoid difficult choices in a recession, but its leaders can handle those choices in ways that are consistent with the culture. In this vein, it's not only what decisions are made but how they are made and communicated that matters. Zappos, the Internet shoe retailer known for its people-oriented culture, recently laid off some of its employees—but it provided them with generous severance packages and six months' worth of health insurance. The CEO explained the rationale behind the layoffs to employees and customers in his blog. "While layoffs are difficult for all parties," one commenter wrote, "I totally respect how you are treating your employees and how you are being transparent about the process."

Changing a dysfunctional culture may be harder, but it is even more urgent. If Detroit's auto companies and some of the big financial services firms are to emerge from the recession as healthy organizations, they will need to develop new values, norms, and behaviors. Any turnaround team jumping into these organizations would focus as much on culture and other organizational matters as on "hard" issues like finance and strategy.

Making the Most of the Crisis

A strong organization isn't optional, something to worry about when the crisis is over. The strength of your organization will greatly affect how well your company can weather the storm. It will greatly affect your chances for growth when the storm passes. Strong organizations identify and focus on their critical decisions—the ones they must make and execute well if they are to succeed. They ensure that their structure and decision roles and processes are set up to facilitate those decisions. They have measures and incentives that make sure people are working toward the right goals. They put the people who can best make and execute those decisions in the right place— even if they have to go out and hire those people.

They also take a good, hard look at their culture, reinforcing the strengths and addressing the weaknesses. And they know that the downturn provides opportunities for change that won't last forever. As somebody in Washington said in early 2009, "A crisis is a terrible thing to waste."

Manage Complexity to Drive Performance Improvement

Downturns reveal a company's weaknesses. An organization that seemed nimble and focused during a period of expansion may be sluggish and ineffectual when faced with declining demand. Its very survival may depend on determining which products are making money, what customers really value, and which organizational bottlenecks are getting in the way of effective action.

One major cause for this sluggishness, in our experience, is complexity—product complexity, organizational complexity, and process complexity. In good times, all three are likely to increase. The costs of complexity are usually hidden, so executives are often unaware of the magnitude of the problem. When the downturn hits, they may be unsure how to tackle it. They often fail to identify the short-term actions that can reduce costs and create flexibility so the company can adjust to new market conditions. They may also neglect the longer-term steps necessary to balance complexity reduction with innovation as the company pulls out of the downturn and begins to grow again.

Managing complexity brings significant benefits in a relatively short time. One of the world's largest natural-resources companies, for example, began its corporate life with only a handful of operations in just a few countries. But as the company grew into a worldwide enterprise, its complexity grew even faster. Costs spiraled out of control, safety procedures were sometimes ignored, and the company's financial performance suffered. A diagnostic assessment revealed huge opportunities for improvement from complexity reduction. The company found that it had no fewer than 483 process improvement projects in the works—and that only 25 would deliver a significant impact. Acting on these and similar findings, the company was able to boost operating income by more than 20 percent.

The "Zero-Base" Approach to Complexity

The challenge with managing complexity, of course, is that some complexity is necessary and advantageous, even in a downturn. For example, country or regional business units are closer to the ground than headquarters is and are more likely to know what customers want. It takes a complex organization to provide enough local autonomy so products or services can be tailored to those customers while still taking advantage of global scale. But that kind of complexity can be vital to sustain sales through a recession. A similar challenge arises when companies struggle to balance complexity and innovation. Adding new products, services, features, and options creates complexity of all sorts. But companies become leaders by offering customers new choices, and in a downturn, innovation may be a company's salvation. (Consider where Apple would be today without iTunes and the iPhone.) The key is not to eliminate complexity but to balance its benefits with its costs.

A useful way of analyzing the level of complexity in your company—and separating complexity that's beneficial from complexity that hurts the business—is to begin from a base of zero. Imagine, for example, that your company produced just one product or service with no options or varieties, sort of like Henry Ford's classic Model T. A manufacturer with only one product would still need a supply chain, a factory, a distribution network, and a sales-and-marketing function. But it could greatly simplify its IT systems, its distribution and sales efforts, and its forecasting. One plant manager with whom we discussed this exercise was bringing in the equivalent of fifteen planes full of parts almost every day just to be sure he could meet the next day's production schedule. In a Model T environment, he noted, "All those costs would disappear instantaneously."

The point of the exercise, of course, isn't to go back to the days of the Model T—which, after all, succumbed to the greater variety offered by General Motors. The point is to determine your zero-complexity costs and then assess the costs of adding variety back in. In a tractor plant, for example, you wouldn't need a scheduling system for one or two models, but you probably would for four. Often the cost curve has just this kind of "knee"—a step change triggered by adding one more model or level of variety—and you can determine whether moving beyond the knee is worth the additional expense. You can also assess the benefits of innovation and determine the focal point where a given innovation overshoots what most customers want and are willing to pay for.

The key task—more essential than ever in a downturn—is to manage these balance points, keeping costs low while maintaining the level of variety and innovation that customers value. For example, you might decide to eliminate individual options and instead offer customers a small number of configurations that include the most popular features. Thus Honda's CRV comes in just 8 configurations and 13 interior/exterior color combinations, for a total of 104 possible build combinations, with no other options available. This is far fewer choices than most cars offer, yet the CRV is the hottest-selling vehicle in its class.

Similar kinds of analyses can diagnose organizational and process complexity. We've found that companies get the best results by attacking product complexity first and organizational complexity next and only then focusing on process complexity. The reason is this: complex processes often reflect unnecessary product variety or poor organizational design. If you attempt to simplify a process without changing product or organizational complexity, you find even more complexity cropping up in some other process area. It's like trying to make a balloon smaller by squeezing one part of it—another part just gets bigger.

Let's take a closer look at each of the three areas of complexity.

Product Complexity

Unnecessary product complexity means offering products, services, or options that relatively few customers want. Most companies, of course, like to give their customers choices. But managers often overestimate buyers' wants and willingness to pay for all those choices. Sometimes, indeed, it's obvious that companies have carried innovation too far. In 2006,

Nestlé introduced a wide array of new variations on its basic Kit Kat candy bar in the United Kingdom, including passion fruit and mango flavors. But the introduction of so many varieties had exactly the opposite effect from what the company hoped: customers were turned off, and sales dropped 18 percent in the course of the year.

A diagnosis of unnecessary product complexity often turns up room for rapid improvement. A major U.S. industrial company, for example, was in its own acute downturn a few years ago: competitive pressures had slashed its operating profits by more than half in less than six months. Analyzing its SKUs, the company found that 80 percent of SKUs contributed only 20 percent of revenues. Needing quick results, it took a three-pronged approach to reducing this complexity:

- *"Drain the swamp."* The company evaluated each SKU through three lenses—customers, operations, and products. Which were most important to major customer segments? Which fit best into the company's operations and product lists? When it dropped an SKU, the company armed its salesforce with alternative products to offer major customers as replacements. These actions enabled it to reduce SKUs by 20 percent immediately—and it ended up adding back only two out of the five hundred that it had eliminated.

- *"Make the best of what's left."* The company then actively attacked complexity in its remaining product portfolio. Within days, it established higher order minimums, longer lead times, and larger production runs. Another quick hit: outsourcing low-volume product families. Over time, the company reassessed other make-versus-buy decisions and established different service levels by customer and product group.

- *"Fix the shop floor."* With a less complex product line, the company set about streamlining its operations. For example, it reduced the number of low-volume products running on high-volume equipment. It cut back on products with inherently high scrap rates or inherently short lead times and products that required specialty materials or processes. It also began altering design specifications so it could make more individual products on the same platform.

These complexity-reduction efforts boosted operating profits by about 2 percent of sales—and about

75 percent of that improvement was achieved in the first year. Even more important, they helped create a nimbler organization, one that could respond rapidly to changes in the marketplace.

Organizational Complexity

As a company expands its product variety or moves into new markets, managers are likely to add organizational complexity. For example, they may try both to maximize scale and to stay close to the customer. Pursuing both these objectives often leads to complex matrix structures, duplicated costs at different levels, and a lack of clear accountabilities. Each decision to add an organizational layer may make sense, but few companies in good times assess the overall impact of these decisions on organizational complexity.

In a downturn, however, the performance burden of an overly complex organization becomes a major disadvantage. We have found three specific areas that provide a quick payoff in terms of nimbleness and the ability to focus.

- *Increase spans and remove layers.* Unnecessary hierarchy contributes to a number of ills, including excessive head count, inflexibility, slower decisions, and a lack of accountability. "Delayering" can help address all these issues.

Companies typically begin by determining the average span of control (the number of employees assigned to any one manager) and the number of layers between the CEO and front-line employees (or between the head of a function and the lowest-level person in the group). They then compare those figures to the competition. A U.S. pharmaceutical company, for example, found that competitors, on average, had 4.2 individuals reporting to each manager in their research function and 6 layers overall between front-line employees and the CEO. Its own organization, by contrast, had only 2 research employees per supervisor and an average of 8 layers from top to bottom. Just getting its organizational structure in line with the competition allowed the company to save as much as $500 million a year.

- *Eliminate decision complexity.* Decision paralysis is another pitfall of complex organizations. (We addressed this point in detail in "Strengthen the Organization.") In brief, however, many companies suffer from unclear decision roles and processes. This is bad in any economic climate, but can be particularly damaging in a downturn. A tool we call

RAPID—for recommend, agree, perform, input, and decide—can help cut through the mess. Take the case of U.K. department store John Lewis. Managers there realized that their product line was too complex—for example, they stocked nearly fifty SKUs of salt-and-pepper mills, while most competitors stocked around twenty. When they tried a new, leaner range of options, however, sales declined. The trouble was this: buyers had expected to maintain the same amount of shelf space. But merchandisers, who put the products on the shelves, had reduced shelf space along with the number of SKUs. By clarifying decision roles between the two groups—who was responsible for making recommendations, for offering input, for signing off on the recommendation, and ultimately for making and implementing the decision—the store was able to maintain the original shelf space with the new range of products. Sales climbed well above original levels.

- *Establish accountability for orphaned costs.* In complex organizations, it may be unclear who is responsible for any given operation, and scrutiny may often be lax. This leads to "orphaned costs": routine costs that are unaccounted for and unmanaged. The magnitude of these costs can be startling. At the natural-resources company we mentioned earlier, investigation determined that there was little or no accountability for approximately 40 percent of the company's overhead costs. Simplifying the organization helped the company attack this problem. For instance, it eliminated redundant finance organizations' operations and clarified the responsibilities of those that remained, ensuring that accountabilities for every cost line were clear.

Each of these measures has its own payoff; together they help create an efficient organization that can move swiftly and focus on the most important activities rather than spinning its wheels.

Process Complexity

Companies that do attempt to manage complexity usually begin with processes, often through efforts such as "lean six sigma." Typically the emphasis is on how companies can execute all their current operations faster and with fewer resources. But that's the wrong place to start. The natural-resources company, remember, had 483 separate process-improvement projects in place. But the whole collection didn't add up to much, because the company had not yet attacked product and organizational complexity. Reducing process complexity should be a company's last step. Here's where to begin the final step:

- *Look for the process improvements that add the most value.* Some processes are obviously critical in any business. A retailer having trouble getting the right mix of products on its shelves, for example, needs to address merchandising right away. In a downturn, the decision about which processes to tackle should be governed in part by how long it will take to yield results. Fixing an inefficient product development process might take years, whereas fixing a poor inventory-management process might take only a few weeks. Companies can then focus on process improvements that promise the biggest returns. The natural-resources company found that 110 of its 483 process-improvement projects were redundant or unjustifiable. Among the remaining 373, it identified 90 that had significant merit. Management then evaluated each of those and narrowed the group down to the 25 initiatives that were likely to generate the most value.

These are now closely tracked by a project management office.

- *Cut through the data clutter.* The natural-resources company also looked into the information and metrics it used to manage the business and discovered that people were drowning in data they weren't using. By determining what kind of management information it truly needed to run its business, the company found it could reduce the volume of reports by 40 percent in one major business unit. That not only accelerated the decision-making process, it also liberated employees to focus on the activities that mattered most to the business and saved $10 million. In cutting through the clutter, you may discover both too much data and a lack of consistency from one data set to another. At a telecommunications company, key metrics like the number of fixed-line customers differed depending on the data source used. And each silo within the business used a different set of data, one that supported its own view of the world. The new CEO at this company had to find out which of the sources of data most closely reflected the truth and determine which methodologies should be used to measure key performance indicators.

That, of course, is the ultimate reward of complexity management. Companies can focus only on the products that are most important to their customers, saving the costs of unwanted production and boosting the margins of the best sellers. By streamlining their organizations they make better, faster decisions, exert tighter control on costs, and can quickly reduce unnecessary head count. Managing process complexity helps companies see where they are overspending and allows them to track performance more effectively.

All these complexity-management efforts help a company become lean and flexible enough to adjust to the changing market conditions in a downturn. It pays off again when the economy improves and a company has stripped out enough complexity to pick up the pace coming out of the downturn.

Streamline G&A

When cost reduction is an urgent priority, one of the first places executives look for savings is general and administrative (G&A) expenses—the cost centers that provide front-line support and back-office functions such as finance, marketing, information technology, and human resources.

There are good reasons that G&A represents such an attractive target. When business is growing, companies tend to add support services. The cost of those services usually doesn't set off alarm bells because profits are healthy and marginal investments are easy to approve. Cost centers may even show apparent correlations between their expanding investments and the improving results of the business. It's like a sailboat that accumulates barnacles: as long as the wind is steady, nobody notices the drag from below the waterline. But when the wind dies, the drag threatens to stall the boat. In a downturn, it becomes painfully apparent that some incremental support services don't contribute enough to sales or earnings, and many executives react with across-the-board cuts in G&A.

This slash-and-burn approach doubtless eliminates some unnecessary expense. But it often destroys value as well. To make their numbers, managers may eliminate activities that really do drive sales and profits. Later, the company realizes it needs at least some of the services those teams were providing. Bit by bit, resources get added back—often just in time to be slashed again in the next downturn.

A Better Way to Streamline

There's a better approach. It can be almost as quick as the slash-and-burn method, and in our experience it produces cost savings that are sustainable, typically in the range of 10 percent to 30 percent. It also improves the productivity and effectiveness of support functions, which in turn helps boost the performance of a company's front line—a powerful advantage in a downturn. We'll describe the steps involved and then look at some examples of how the approach works in practice.

Invert the Pyramid

The approach begins with what we call inverting the pyramid. The usual organizational pyramid shows front-line managers and employees—the people who deal with customers and perform mission-critical operations such as sales or service—at the base. Support functions are somewhere in the middle, and senior management is at the top. Tipping the pyramid upside down emphasizes the importance of the people who actually provide the products and services that customers value. Below them are the support and back-office functions that help the front line deliver the goods or services. At the bottom is senior management, whose fundamental job is to help the rest of the organization do its work effectively.

The inverted pyramid provides a kind of acid test for support services: Which of HR's many activities, for example, help put talented, well-trained people in a company's critical positions? Which of IT's activities solve the problems that are getting in the way of delivering value to the customer? Using the inverted pyramid, executives can determine which support services are essential to the front line, where the company makes its money each day.

Reduce, Redesign, and Restructure

There are three ways to maximize front-line benefits while eliminating unnecessary support expense. The key is to understand which services should be reduced, which should be redesigned, and which should be restructured.

To *reduce*, companies can clarify what support functions are expected to deliver and eliminate non-essential activities. The key is to start with the internal customers and their demand for services, rather than service providers and what they currently supply. Some companies use internal pricing mechanisms to help executives see which services front-line managers really want, based on what they're willing to pay for. *Redesign* requires companies to scrutinize the processes that deliver support services. They can streamline some—often by automating certain steps—and purchase better or lower-cost inputs for others. *Restructuring* usually involves consolidation or outsourcing. The goal is to ensure that support services are located and organized in such a way that they can perform most effectively at lowest cost.

Run Support Functions Based on Productivity and Output, Not Only Costs

Minimizing costs is rarely a business's sole objective, because some costs create value that customers are willing to pay for. It's the same with G&A: minimizing costs for every function is seldom the right answer, because companies need to invest in support functions that make their front lines more productive. When management teams focus on effectiveness as well as efficiency, they usually get the best results.

What can you expect from this approach? Typically, a combination of reduction, redesign, and restructuring can save about 20 percent of G&A costs, although some companies save more and some less, depending on their starting point. In our experience, reduction of use usually accounts for about 25 percent of total savings; redesign, 35 percent; and restructuring, about 40 percent. And by focusing on effectiveness and efficiency together, these cost savings can be sustained.

Let's move on to the examples.

Tailoring Support by Product Family

Inflexible back-office cuts can impose one-size-fits-all procedures on a company's production and marketing activities. That's unlikely to help a company adapt to an ever more competitive marketplace.

Consider the case of an office products company. Faced with fierce competition from overseas suppliers and big-box stores hawking private-label goods, this company knew it needed to improve its performance. Part of the answer lay in cutting costs dramatically to allow for more competitive pricing. So the company centralized support functions, eliminating what had been a high level of duplication across its business units.

But while lowering costs was essential to greater efficiency, the company also saw a big opportunity to improve its performance through more effective marketing and R&D. Some of its customers bought primarily on price. So in certain product categories, *reduce* was a key lever as the company slashed support spending to compete with very low-cost, private-label goods. But other customers valued innovation and sought out some of the company's brand-name products. In these high-value categories, the company actually increased its investments in R&D and marketing support to bring innovation to the customers who cared most about it. Finance staff were key in analyzing which features would enable market share gains along with high profit margins.

In most cost-cutting campaigns, R&D, marketing, support, and finance staff would be in the crosshairs. But for this company, an across-the-board cut would have been a mistake. By segmenting its customers and product categories, it was able to cut costs judiciously, which resulted in an overall boost in productivity and sales in its core product lines. That led to an improved cost structure and some of the strongest economics in the industry.

Eliminating Bottlenecks

Speed is paramount in turbulent times. But ineffective support services can create bottlenecks that slow organizations down. Consider the experience of one international entertainment company. The company was hoping to capitalize on its popularity by adding shows on its global tours. But to its dismay, it found that costs were rising faster than revenues. Adding more shows threatened to flatten margins instead of generating the profits that might be expected from spreading costs across more output.

The problem turned out to be twofold. First, the company had a tangle of back-office services, like finance and HR, that were duplicated for each show. In effect, a mini-back office, including a financial controller, a dedicated HR staffer, and so on, hit the road with the performers for every show. The back office provided services, but the incremental cost was debilitating. Second, many crucial support services, from costume making to casting, were world class and were treated as such—quality always came first. This was hardly surprising: the company's core asset was its ability to put on unique, high-quality events that drew rave reviews and commanded a premium ticket price. But nobody was paying attention to the efficiency of the back-office systems.

Creating a back-office structure more amenable to profitable, sustainable growth meant *redesigning* much of what was already in place. As a creative enterprise, however, the company had to examine closely which processes could be redesigned (and how) without disrupting the artistry that so appealed to customers. It also had to respect what needed to remain inviolate—costly but essential parts of the high-quality production process such as expensive props or staging installations.

Some of the solutions were obvious, such as centralizing and streamlining the finance and HR functions. Originally, despite the distributed nature of the finance function, transactions for as little as $20 had had to be signed off centrally. Simply processing the transaction could cost more than the amount being processed. To resolve this issue, the company provided its staff with credit cards for small purchases.

Other solutions were less obvious. HR, for instance, had invested heavily in creating a database of candidates for the most skilled and versatile positions in its shows. It spent less time collecting names of less-skilled players. When the company looked more closely at absentee rates and backup depth, however, it realized that the greatest need for replacements due to injuries or illness was among the rank-and-file performers, while the most-skilled roles had more backups than were necessary. That meant there was room to invest less in recruiting for starring-role understudies while still ensuring that backups were always available. HR could focus more where it was most needed, while spending less overall.

Costume making was another area of opportunity. At first, the costume shop was off limits to the efficiency drive. The craftsman ethic was strong, and costume makers proudly sewed their garments from hand-dyed fabric. Creating and repairing costumes was labor intensive, however, and skilled artisans were in short supply. Processing twice the volume—the expectation in the growth strategy—was out of the question. So the company analyzed which costume elements were commodity items and which were truly unique. Eventually it was able to outsource production of several commodity items without compromising overall quality, thereby eliminating another bottleneck. The show could go on—more often than before and with higher profitability.

Improving the Productivity
of the Front Line

Sometimes back-office processes actively interfere with mission-critical, customer-facing activities. No company can afford that when times are hard. It's one reason why inverting the pyramid and listening closely to the front line are so important. Consider the approach taken by Kyobo Life, a Korean financial services company that took quick, practical steps to *restructure* its customer support operation and to *redesign* some of its processes to make the salesforce more productive.

Kyobo was an early adopter of the Internet sales channel in Korea. It began selling automobile insurance policies on the Web in 1999. It also operated branch offices where salespeople could meet directly with customers. At the branches, bringing a higher level of efficiency and effectiveness required more finesse. Each branch had thirty to fifty sales agents advising clients on investment options and insurance products. But the same agents were also responsible for customer support, and the company's incentives actually encouraged them to divide their time between sales and support. Sales productivity lagged. When Kyobo studied the situation, it discovered that the average agent spent 60 percent of his or her time on support—a back-office function—and only 40 percent on selling.

One way out of this box might have been to change the incentive system, so that expensive, specialized sales agents earned more for selling than for customer support. But Kyobo's business would suffer if it simply reduced support. The solution instead began with inverting the pyramid to understand what support services the front-line agents required to boost productivity. With that perspective in mind, Kyobo's sales managers proposed investing in a customer call center that would handle both customer support and lead generation. Call-center staff would pass along the leads to the sales agents, splitting the commissions. To be sure, Kyobo had to invest in training the call-center staff. But the restructuring plan energized the sales-force and made it more productive. Some "mission critical" and "need to be live" elements of customer service were left with the sales force.

G&A offers companies many opportunities for low-ering costs and improving performance quickly. The current downturn is likely to be lengthy, and a focus on G&A effectiveness as well as efficiency can help com-panies survive. But the downturn won't last forever. When it ends, companies will need to take their foot off the brake and step on the gas pedal. Wholesale G&A cuts are likely to slow results now and get in the way of rapid acceleration later. Smart strategic mea-sures, the kind that boost effectiveness while increas-ing efficiency, will help a company both survive turbulence and accelerate out of it.

Tightly Manage Cash Flows
and Liquidity

Navigating through turbulence at thirty thousand feet is different than at three thousand feet. Up high, pilots have more options. They can maneuver around approaching storms or reduce their speed for a smoother ride. If fuel is running low, they can scout for the best runway to touch down safely and plan their next moves. Closer to the ground, everything changes. Storms are unavoidable, reaction times shrink, and options evaporate. Staying aloft requires quick and accurate decisions based on an immediate grasp of the resources available.

It's much the same for business leaders flying through major economic turbulence. Knowing your altitude in terms of financial strength and flexibility is crucial. Earnings statements provide one vital measure of financial health. In a downturn, though, cash flow and liquidity analyses serve as even more precise altimeters, fuel gauges, and radar systems. They provide a close view of how resources actually flow through the system and which product lines, customer relationships, and vendors are generating cash rather than consuming it—key data that helps corporate pilots steer more precisely and confidently.

Until recently, most senior executives regarded managing cash and liquidity as tactical functions, a fairly mundane set of activities that could be left to administrative managers. That's changed. As the global financial crisis has choked off credit, cash management has become strategic. Companies with weak operating cash flows are finding it more difficult to secure outside funding, making those companies more dependent on operating cash at a time when cash flows are harder than ever to generate. The resulting spiral can bring down even the largest global players.

On the other hand, companies that aggressively manage cash and liquidity—and use the perspective and the data that come with it to gain forward visibility—have opportunities to prosper in turbulence. Wal-Mart, for instance, is aggressively managing its resources to take advantage of others' weaknesses. To generate cash, the company has cut capital expenditures, halted a stock buyback program, and trimmed inventories. It has shifted cash from opening new stores to remodeling existing ones. This sort of cash discipline has sharpened operations and allowed Wal-Mart to keep cutting prices without damaging its business.

Many senior executives have come to recognize the importance of understanding in detail how resources flow through the enterprise when the margins for error are severely limited. Downside scenarios informed by cash flow and liquidity measures can show management teams how much cash they need to preserve and protect the business under different conditions. The right models can reveal choke points and opportunities to improve processes. They can also highlight differences in efficiency between various product lines, customer channels, and vendor relationships, suggesting which levers to focus on and when to pull them. Turned outward and focused on the cash flows of competitors, customers, and vendors, these analyses provide a powerful understanding of which rivals are vulnerable, which customers are strongest, and which vendors might not survive.

The immediate opportunity is to use cash and capital resources more efficiently. But the value of this approach builds with time. The accumulated data helps companies to spot patterns and understand what drives variances in liquidity and how those variances flow through to the profit-and-loss statement. With this perspective and the detail that underlies it, companies can start to predict the business obstacles created by the peaks and valleys, giving management teams valuable time to respond before their options run out. The overarching objective is to develop enough forward visibility to manage effectively through even a sustained period of turbulence.

Staying Aloft

When a storm hits, every company benefits from a sharper focus on cash flows and liquidity. But the call to action will be different based on what the analyses show. Cash-strapped companies need to focus on defensive actions—slashing inventories, clamping down on expenses, and cutting back on compensation and benefits. Healthy companies with cash reserves like Wal-Mart have more strategic options.

Managing cash effectively is fairly straightforward. The key is to do it rigorously and systematically. In our experience, a critical first step is implementing a practical thirteen-week cash flow tool that starts from the bottom of an enterprise and builds upward, showing what's flowing into and out of each business segment on a weekly and monthly basis. The idea is to capture real-time information on flows and compare them to budgeted amounts. Persistent variances signal problems that can be addressed before it is too late.

The visibility that accompanies this kind of discipline can be powerful. One large high-tech industrial group in Europe recently found itself pressed for cash by the global slowdown, despite having secured a large line of credit one year earlier. The payment cycles in several older industrial equipment businesses had been stretched out as sales slowed and customers struggled with payments. That was needlessly tying up cash in mature parts of the business that had the least growth potential. Worse, the situation was starving capital from a promising solar power unit, which needed investment to capture a major competitive opportunity.

The key was breaking down the company's net working capital requirements by business line and function to determine how long cash was locked up, from initial acquisition of raw materials to the last customer payment. When it compared those cash cycles against the competition, the company discovered a wide gap in the efficiency of its accounts receivable, inventories, and accounts payable in key segments. Rivals were collecting faster, stretching out their own payments, and aggressively managing inventories.

The company determined that closing the gap could free up $350 million to $600 million in cash.

That would provide money to fortify the mature businesses against the downturn and capital to invest in the promising solar business. The moves were not radical: cracking down on receivables collection, enhancing payables terms with suppliers, and managing inventories better by increasing just-in-time delivery and shortening the work-in-process cycle. The key was focusing managers' attention by improving the organization's access to information.

Focusing attention on which levers can be pulled to the greatest effect is one of the key benefits of cash flow and liquidity analysis. Many companies have discovered in the downturn that their reliance on free-flowing, cheap capital covered up a host of problems. One major cosmetics company, for instance, spent years financing inefficient customer channels without running into problems. But when money got tight, the high cost of loose working capital management showed up quickly. High-, medium-, or low-volume accounts were all treated the same. Contract incentives were built to encourage orders, not sell-through. When business slowed, the cash cycle lengthened, dramatically exposing the highly leveraged company to a liquidity squeeze. An analysis of all the inputs—including invested balance sheet capital—produced a surprising result: the company was spending $1.86 for each dollar of sales. Investing more intelligently by focusing on the cost of sell-through, instead of just pipeline filling, promised as much as $800 million in freed-up capital.

Analyzing the cash flow and liquidity of competitors and customers also provides powerful competitive information that can be used strategically. One global consumer products firm, for instance, used a downturn in its business to win new customers with lower prices, convinced that its main rival's weak balance sheet and lax cash management practices would leave it unwilling or unable to respond. After doing a thorough analysis of its rival's liquidity, the company set prices low enough to attract new business and keep its plants humming. That crimped the profitability of its main business, but top management reasoned the company could afford some softness in that division because it was diversified into other product lines. Not so its competitor. Lost business upset the relationships between fixed and variable costs and destroyed the profitability of the rival company's plants. With no focus on managing cash or liquidity, the company failed to respond with lower prices until it was caught in a severe liquidity crisis. Betting on the strength of its balance sheet and the weakness of its rivals gave the consumer products firm enough confidence to make a bold strategic move when others were retrenching.

Seeing the Future

The short-term view of how cash flows through the business enhances long-term perspective. With the information on how your business behaves over a period of time, you can model scenarios that trigger liquidity problems and show what business obstacles those squeezes create. Facing the current economic shock, for instance, top executives can model what would happen to their business if the downturn lasts another six months, lasts another year, or gets even worse. Forewarned is forearmed. By tracking the way changes to their assumptions affect cash flow, management teams can anticipate and react much faster, knowing which actions will make the greatest difference.

Consider the process used by one auto rental company concerned that heavy inventory costs left it highly vulnerable in the last economic downturn. The company was contractually obligated to take billions of dollars worth of cars from the auto manufacturers each year. Managing that inventory efficiently required a detailed understanding of the working capital implications for each class of car rented in every conceivable situation.

The company generated reams of data illuminating key factors such as which regions were strongest and weakest, where lucrative business travelers congregated most, which airport locations generated the most traffic, and how seasonality changed the mix. Management also ran thirteen-week cash flow analyses to figure out how cash moved through the system and how it ebbed and flowed in various precincts based on business conditions. After collecting data for eight months, the company had enough information to start building scenarios that modeled cash flow and earnings changes in different macroeconomic environments. Right away, it became obvious that management had several available levers to pull to save cash and shore up operations if business conditions worsened.

One of them involved the company's preferred-customer desk, an amenity designed to lure frequent travelers by allowing them to pick any car in the company's fleet for a set price. From a marketing standpoint, the desk was a big win and a competitive advantage. But from a cash flow perspective, it was a mess: every model in the fleet had its own working capital implications, yet preferred customers paid a single fixed price. Despite the marketing punch, the math didn't work.

Tracking cash flow weekly for the short term and monthly for the longer term provided a deep understanding of these relationships and enabled the company to envision the kind of fix it would need to implement when business tightened. By understanding the behavior of their most lucrative business customers and knowing the cash cycle of each class of automobile, top managers could adjust the fleet so that the company offered top choice only at the most important locations. At noncore rental offices, either the preferred desk would be eliminated or management would clamp down hard on the number of choices available to customers. The model anticipated that some customers would leave, but it would also free up $200 million to $300 million in cash to invest elsewhere.

Building an Integrated View

Scenarios like these help companies gain an integrated perspective on how operations affect the balance sheet. They highlight how actions by divisional heads, plant managers, and other line managers have a direct effect on cash flow and the balance sheet. Scenarios help develop policies for cash clearing, inventory targets, days sales outstanding, and other working capital items. The goal is to make sure these are defined, not just left to the discretion of individual managers.

By providing a view of which parts of the business are most efficient and lucrative, cash flow and liquidity analyses lead naturally to analyzing returns on capital across various businesses, essentially tying together the balance sheet and the profit-and-loss statement. Those analyses help managers decide where capital should flow to maximize overall returns, avoiding the common impulse to spread investment across a company evenly, regardless of where it is doing the most good.

Longer term, managing for cash flow helps executives to hone a company's strategy based on a full picture of how the business is performing week to week. That can help make informed choices and free up capital to invest opportunistically throughout the downturn.

With skillful and constant adjustments by corporate "pilots," strong, erratic winds can also lift a company. In that sense, cash flow and liquidity analyses can serve not only to guide a company's strategy, but also to increase its thrust.

Turbocharge Sales

When business conditions are harsh, you need every dollar of revenue you can find. Unfortunately, so do your competitors—who seem willing to do anything for a buck. You don't want to buy business indiscriminately at discount rates. But you also aren't willing to sacrifice market share to more-aggressive competitors. So how is it possible to *gain* share without giving away the store?

One powerful way to shore up sales and margin in a downturn is to make your salesforce more effective. A few years ago, GE Commercial Finance added $300 million of profitable new business in twelve months by restructuring and refocusing its sales organization. Those improvements have helped GE Commercial Finance weather the storm better than many in the hard-hit financial services sector. More recently, a mid-sized network equipment company reversed three straight years of declining revenue and improved its gross margin, primarily by revamping its sales efforts. A more focused selling operation, in other words, can increase productivity and work wonders for the top and bottom lines when both are under pressure.

What are the right moves? The key is a numbers-driven approach to boosting your sales organization's effectiveness. The methodology is summed up in a framework we call TOPSales: Targeted offerings, Optimized tools and procedures, Performance management, and Sales resource deployment. It provides executives with a set of practical levers they can systematically apply to increase sales and margins. The following four tactics—all based on the TOPSales approach—will help you ring the cash register now.

Targeted Offerings: Create a "Heat Map"— and Double Down on the Hot Spots

Every company has its best customers. These customers are the most profitable and typically the most loyal. What you offer them—the product or service, the brand, the customer experience—is exactly what they want. Sales from such customers produce "good revenue," the kind that's predictable and profitable, and holds possibilities for further expansion. Bad revenue, in contrast, comes from customers that don't value your core business proposition. They require excessive customization, complexity, or discounting, and they cause the sales management team to lose strategic focus. Tempting though it may be, no company can afford bad revenue, with its explicit and hidden costs.

Companies typically identify their best customers by analyzing win rates, revenue, relative market share, and profitability among customer segments. Economic downturns demand additional measures. Which customers will still be strong and continue buying in spite of the downturn? Which have strong cash positions, good access to credit, or both? It is also vital to understand which companies *should* be your best customers, even if they haven't been buying from you in the past. In a down market, when many companies are re-evaluating their suppliers, opportunities arise to steal share from a distracted competitor. Slowdowns affect industries, regions, and individual companies differently. You need to know not just who your best customers were in the past but who your best customers will be now and in the future, and how this new perspective affects the potential size of your customer segments.

High-potential customers are the hot spots in an otherwise cooling economy. Once you have a sense of who they are, you can draw a "heat map" of the market to guide your sales efforts. Managers and reps can identify and sell the specific combinations of products or services best suited to these customers' needs in a downturn. For example, selling campaigns should be created around those that offer productivity improvements, those that provide a quick return on investment, or those that can be covered by a customer's operating budget rather than by its constrained capital budget. Everyone who interacts with customers can concentrate his or her efforts on the hot spots, with the goal of retaining profitable buyers and generating demand. A few months ago, for example, a broadcasting company refocused its advertising sales team on a few key segments, including health-care providers, which appeared to be less affected by the downturn, and specialty retailers, which desperately needed advertising to counter declines in consumer spending. After just two months, sales in the broadcaster's two test regions were up 90 percent and 450 percent.

That kind of targeting pays off, of course, only if reps are held to tight guidelines on pricing. Pricing is the subject of another chapter, so we won't go into detail here. But in a downturn, sales managers need to be particularly aware of potential profit erosion due to price leakage. Carefully calibrated strategic promotions aimed at maintaining share in key market segments may make sense. But discounting and other forms of trade spending can go unchecked without close attention from management. One appliance company found that dealer discounts, display and price promotions, and rebates had unintentionally reduced its average realized price to only 57 percent of net market price. After analysis, the company was able both to reduce overall discounting and to redirect some of the dollars to high-growth accounts. The result was a 20 percent increase in earnings before interest and taxes (EBIT). Targeted offerings enable these kinds of fast adjustments, concentrating resources and effort on the accounts that will contribute most when sales are dropping or profitability is under pressure.

Optimized Tools and Procedures: Put Muscle into Pipeline Management

In a downturn, sales cycles lengthen, sometimes considerably. Prospects express interest but won't commit. Customers commit verbally but won't place the order. Cash is tight everywhere, and procurement specialists move slowly. Sales reps may believe they have full pipelines. To managers, however, the pipes seem full of molasses. There just isn't much business coming out the tap.

Close, disciplined pipeline management attuned to the heat map can help improve win rates for the business that is flowing. Sales managers and reps have three essential tasks in this area: screening each sales opportunity; ensuring that high-priority projects get the marketing, selling, and executive support they need; and tracking progress against goals.

- *Screening.* A heat map has obvious advantages for account planning, but it also lets you dissect the existing pipeline. Managers can screen out the opportunities that don't fit the map. They can focus reps' efforts on those that do fit. With longer sales cycles, your selling resources will be stretched across more accounts, and you have to make certain they are aimed at the right targets. Sales managers also need to ensure that reps have honest assessments of when they expect sales to close. The key here is careful forecasting, tracking, and discussion of major opportunities. Even if elapsed time increases, the company should have internal benchmarks on conversion rates from one stage to the next and historical win rates relative to major competitors—and should apply those benchmarks rigorously.

- *Support.* Many companies have realized that a downturn is a good time to switch to a more consultative selling process in order to discover and address customer opportunities that are harder for less astute competitors to tackle.

Marketing and sales-support materials used in a consultative process can be tailored closely to client needs. The broadcasting company's sales reps, for instance, relied on market research and messages designed for each targeted segment. In consultative sessions, the reps offered clients customized "flights" of commercials specifying lengths, frequencies, and times of day, along with cross-platform (online) advertising opportunities—all with the aim of maximizing the ads' impact on consumers.

- *Tracking.* Every company tracks prospective sales as well as deals that have closed. Few push sales tracking deep into the rhythm of the organization. Companies such as GE, IBM, and Cisco have customized "digital cockpits" that enable quick, regular pipeline X-rays and analyses. The demand for current information is particularly acute in a downturn, because the sales organization may need to react rapidly to changes in the marketplace. One computer industry executive told us, "The sales cadence and pipeline management system that was institutionalized around Y2K really helped us in the 2001 crash. It was a key enabler for us to perform as well as we did."

There are many automated tools on the market that can facilitate tracking. The growing popularity of software-as-a-service means that companies can buy automated tools on a pay-as-you-go basis. That may be an attractive option when cash is scarce. What matters most, though, isn't the technology or tools you choose, it's the management processes and disciplines that put the technology to work. These include systematic channeling of leads to reps; routine, detailed account and pipeline discussions; and meticulous tracking of customers' readiness to purchase as well as their current cash-and-credit positions. Some companies create a "Deal War Room" when turbulence hits their industries to ensure this kind of discipline is applied consistently, with clearly defined roles for each function to play in driving revenue.

Performance Management: Scope Territories and Quotas for a Downturn

Traditionally, sales managers have defined territories and set quotas based on a combination of history, gut instinct, and mandates from headquarters. If headquarters expected revenue growth of 10 percent, every rep's quota would be set 10 percent higher than last year's. That approach no longer works well, even in the best of times. Forward-looking companies are adopting more scientific techniques for managing the salesforce.

At Aggreko North America, a division of the U.K.–based equipment rental company, executives gather regional data on the critical business factors that influence each of the company's markets—oil refining, home construction, and so on—and then calculate the firm's share of each market to set goals for growth. Armed with this data, area sales managers develop a view of territories, accounts, and quotas for individual reps by multiplying potential market size by target shares for each market. An iterative process between the local reps and senior management ensures that expectations for individual salespeople are both realistic and in line with overall corporate objectives. The new numbers-driven approach helped Aggreko boost salesforce productivity by 90 percent in one year.

When the economy is struggling, the need for accurate data of this sort is even more acute. Do territories correspond appropriately to the heat map, or are some productive reps left out in the cold? Are quotas realistic in light of the new conditions? The network equipment company that turned around its revenue decline had been pursuing fifteen different industry segments. But its heat map showed that five of those segments accounted for most of its revenue and profits. So it redesigned territories and reset quotas accordingly.

Companies can develop scorecards for both reps and managers to help them track their own performance. A rep's scorecard could include metrics such as the company's share of the customer's wallet in the current conditions; the rep's progress toward quota; the health of the pipeline at each stage; and even the quality of account plans for selected strategic accounts from the heat map. Managers' cards can include overall margin and rep turnover (both wanted and unwanted), as well as the individual metrics for the reps they supervise.

Sales Resource Deployment: Get the Mix of Resources Right for Today's Conditions

When customers are wary of buying, sales managers face two critical challenges. One is to maximize the time reps can spend in front of customers, explaining the benefits of what they are selling. The other is to keep overall sales costs under tight control. Effective deployment of sales resources can help with both objectives.

To maximize face time, check the heat map: the hot spots show the customers most likely to buy. That's where you need your best reps—and you need them out there selling, not traveling or doing paperwork. Measure the time that reps spend in front of customers compared to total time. If it's less than what you think it should be, or less than benchmarks for your industry, consider channeling some of the reps' administrative functions to support staff, rearranging territories to reduce transit time, or simplifying the systems that the reps are expected to deal with. A few years ago, sales executives at Cisco Systems set a goal of reducing reps' non-selling time by a few hours each week and charged the IT department with making it happen. The subsequent improvements in Cisco's sales-support systems streamlined the administrative tasks required of sales reps and helped to generate several hundred million dollars in additional revenue.

A downturn may also require companies to streamline and rationalize their salesforces. With the right approach, that becomes a powerful lever to refocus the salesforce and boost productivity. Most companies use a variety of sales channels: enterprise or other direct sales, telephone sales, dealers or value-added resellers, and the Internet. In many industries, a combination of mergers or acquisitions and ongoing product extensions has created a need for specialists to complement the generalists in the field. Detailed information about the behavior and profitability of customer segments and microsegments from the heat map, as well as data about the productivity of existing selling efforts, allow sales executives to decide how best to deploy these different resources. To keep costs low, a company can beef up its telesales operation and replace underperforming in-field reps. Aggreko North America, for instance, now directs inquiries about commodity rentals to the Internet or handles them through telesales, while inquiries about large consultative projects are sent to specialized sales reps.

A downturn is also a good time to increase your use of partners. The network equipment company mentioned earlier boosted its revenue partly by focusing business development and marketing efforts with a few select partners. For example, it bundled a networking solution with PCs and servers from one OEM that was targeting the same industry segment. This was no small effort: the partners developed joint marketing collateral, events, training, and refined incentives for each organization, not to mention joint pipeline planning. But it paid dividends; the network equipment company grew its sales with that partner threefold in just nine months.

Preparing for Recovery

No downturn lasts forever. When the recovery comes, your sales organization should be positioned to capitalize on pent-up demand. Companies that win during and after turbulence often recruit top sales talent from competitors or may even pursue acquisitions and integrate the acquired company's best sales reps with their own.

In either case, the TOPSales approach helps position the salesforce for high performance. It focuses sales teams on robust data-gathering operations and then uses that data to set goals and quotas, manage territories and pipelines, and ensure consistency in processes and priorities. It helps ensure that you have the right mix of specialists and generalists, and that your reps are trained to sell products and services tailored to what companies need in a downturn. Companies can no longer afford to rely on the persuasive or relationship-building powers of a small group of stars with native sales talent.

The steps outlined will help you get started on the process while you're navigating turbulence. Every business confronting a downturn needs to sustain revenue and margin, and astute management of your salesforce will improve your performance in both areas.

Price for Today and Tomorrow

Confronted by weakening sales and excess capacity, management teams often resort to cutting prices. It's easy to see why. Price cuts are quicker and easier to implement than, say, introducing new products or improving service levels. Customers often respond immediately to lowered prices. A swift uptick in sales can reinforce executives' belief that they did the right thing.

But there's a reason promotional price cuts are sometimes called "management heroin." Price cuts are addictive. Customers quickly develop a craving for big discounts and an aversion to full prices. Companies grow accustomed to the boost in volume and hesitate to raise prices to previous levels for fear that revenues will crater. In a deep recession, when the first goal is survival, some businesses have no option but to cut prices aggressively. But even relatively strong companies experiment with heavy discounts and then wake up to find themselves hooked.

Is there an alternative? The truth is, most companies do need to lower prices in a downturn, whether they sell primarily to businesses or to consumers. Demand is down, yet fixed capacity and costs haven't changed much. So the laws of supply and demand exert strong downward pressure on prices. Still, the range of outcomes can vary widely in both the short term and the long term. What matters most is how effectively companies manage pricing.

Unfortunately, yesterday's pricing textbook isn't much help with today's conditions. A sharp, prolonged downturn creates a volatile new environment, altering the behavior of both customers and competitors in unpredictable ways. Companies have to act quickly, even though solid information is hard to come by. And pricing decisions made now are likely to affect customers' perceptions for a long time to come. Few companies in any industry can say, "We'll lower prices today and raise them tomorrow"—at least not without risking a severe customer backlash.

In our experience, companies that get pricing right manage it at three levels. They create a pricing *strategy* that fully supports their broader objectives and positioning. They set prices on individual *products* to reflect value to both buyer and seller. And they deploy disciplined *tactics* to manage the aspects of the transaction that most affect profitability. A severe downturn presents challenges on all three levels. Pricing strategy must address stark differences between the right short-term answers and the long-term health of the business. Pricing of individual products needs to reflect dramatic changes in the ways customers make purchasing decisions. Tactics must be carefully designed and choreographed to let companies execute quickly without losing control.

In a normal business environment the best course is almost always to map out your strategy first, then to set prices for individual products, and finally to design the suite of tactics that will allow you to execute profitably. But in a recession, time is compressed, and tactical decisions take on new importance and urgency. So we'll start there.

Tactics: Speed Is Crucial—But So Is Control

Customer behavior, markets, and competitors' actions can all change quickly in a downturn. Executives find that previous assumptions are obsolete and they must act faster than ever to adapt. But when companies accelerate tactical pricing moves without accurate information about the real effects of those moves, they can lose control of the prices customers actually pay. The most effective companies typically take two steps to avoid this danger: (1) they quickly assess the impact of pricing moves by gathering lots of fast, fresh point-of-sale data, and (2) they maximize control by identifying and managing the hidden sources of revenue leakage.

Gather Fast, Ground-Level Information on the Impact of Your Pricing Tactics

Most companies rely on a host of discounts, promotions, and other pricing tactics to boost sales and earnings. In a downturn, it becomes essential to analyze which really work and which waste money.

The actions flowing from this kind of analysis not only shore up the bottom line, they also lay the groundwork for more effective pricing in the future. One specialty retailer we worked with, for example, carried fifty thousand SKUs per store—as much variety as a large supermarket—and relied on promotions to drive a significant portion of sales. When the retailer put its promotions under the analytic microscope, however, it found that discounts on some items had virtually no effect on sales. It also discovered that some forms of promotional pricing were far more profitable than others, even if the costs were similar. Customers loved two-for-the-price-of-one offers, for instance, yet were less impressed by 50 percent–off sales.

The retailer also relearned the importance of seasonality in pricing tactics. Discounting a highly seasonal product—patio furniture in New England, say—at the very beginning of the selling season typically attracted a large number of shoppers looking for bargains. Discounting the same item at any other time of year was essentially fruitless, because shoppers were more willing to pay full price. After analysis, the store modified or eliminated only 10 percent of its promotions overall. But that 10 percent yielded a boost in profitability of 15 to 20 percent, while sales volume declined less than 2 percent.

The faster you can gather this data and act on it, the more likely you can stay in touch with changing customer needs and preferences. One food-products company, for instance, built quantitative tools that analyzed sales data from competitors along with its own operations every week. Managers could track the relationships between price points and volume and spot the gaps between the company and its competitors. They linked promotional tactics to sales volume, compared actual to predicted results, and adjusted their demand models on a weekly basis. In an industry where monthly sales data and quarterly adjustments were standard, the weekly data helped the company adapt much faster than competitors to changing conditions.

Discipline Your Selling Efforts to Eliminate Leakage

A downturn increases the pressure on employees to chase or protect volume at any price. Freight terms given by the logistics department, credit terms authorized by finance, free services and accessories authorized by customer-care agents—all can create layers of overlapping discounts and hidden leaks that drain away profits. The faster and more aggressively you move on pricing tactics, the more important it is to reassert control.

A European machinery manufacturer did just that, with remarkable results. Like many producers of complex products, this company typically realized net prices that were about 55 percent of list. But those discounts came from a wide range of sources. A product costing €100 might carry several on-invoice discounts totaling €35. Off-invoice terms or incentives might be worth another €10. Managers had no way of identifying why a particular product was selling for less than list, and had little control over which people in the organization were authorized to provide discounts. Front-line salespeople in particular offered substantial incentives without oversight by senior management.

To address the problem, the company sent out a short e-mail survey to its sales force asking about their discounting and contracting practices. The survey results, along with input from the finance department, allowed managers to simulate the impact of promotional activity and establish guidelines to maximize return on investment. The company also built tracking systems to capture off-invoice trade spending and aggregate that data at the account level to ensure that the company was investing in the most valuable accounts. The result was an increase in earnings before interest and taxes of nearly 20 percent.

Maintaining control of pricing execution requires clear direction to front-line employees about what's allowed and disciplined processes to find and remedy unauthorized behavior. For big-ticket items, managers need to set clear guidelines for sales scripts and allowable price ranges. They need to have a well-developed escalation process for decisions that fall outside company pricing guidelines. Managers can also ratchet up discipline by tying both sales force and channel compensation to price realization. It's hard enough maintaining margins even in the best of circumstances; in a recession no company can afford uncontrolled discounting.

Product: Listen to the Customer, Not Your Own Uneasiness

Falling demand in turbulent times triggers a cascade of list-price declines and deep discounts off list. Yet many companies lower prices too aggressively or too broadly because they fail to answer two key questions: *Why* is demand falling? and *Where* is it falling most? Answering these questions requires managers to get inside their customers' heads.

Why Is Demand Falling?

In a downturn, some consumers and businesses cut back because they just don't have the money to spend. Many more prospective customers have the money but feel uncertain about the future. Both factors show up in the price declines that hit the transportation sector, for example, where average prices fell roughly 13 percent in the first few months of 2009. So, which factor should get the greatest attention?

Spooked consumers won't buy more until they feel that it is safe to do so, or until they decide that prices have dropped as far as they're going to. A company needs to understand its customers well enough to know which of these factors is more important. If your customers can afford to buy but are nervous about doing so, lowering prices may not be the right way to help them overcome inertia. Rather, companies can find ways—by combining pricing with other marketing efforts—to send the message that buying is a low-risk decision.

Take cars, for example. Plummeting employment doubtless contributed to the sharp drop in auto sales in 2008 and early 2009. But *fear* of job loss probably kept many more potential buyers out of dealer showrooms. Cars are a big-ticket item, and most customers can delay purchases by a year or two.

In response, auto companies typically slash prices in a downturn. Most of the big players, desperate for sales, did it this time around. But Hyundai took a different tack. Recognizing that its customers weren't likely to respond to the usual rebates or incentives, the Korean car maker announced a plan that would allow customers who lost their jobs to return a new car. The reasoning: A fully employed customer can afford the full-price car nearly as easily as the discounted car. But a customer fearing layoffs is more likely to hold off on big purchases. The strategy is powerful because it addresses what goes on inside a customer's head, not what goes on in an economics textbook. It carries some risks, but it is not as risky as watching sales plummet—and indeed, Hyundai's sales were up nearly 5 percent in the first several weeks of 2009, compared with the same period in 2008. Overall auto sales, meanwhile, had dropped 40 percent.

Where Is Demand Falling Most?

Rather than relying on highly visible across-the-board discounting, sophisticated pricers find ways to lower average prices in highly selective ways. Almost every company's business contains "pockets" of real variance in demand—customer segments, geographies, product lines, occasions of use, and so on. In our experience, most companies underestimate how many of these pockets can be addressed effectively through targeted pricing.

Faced with a big fourth-quarter sales drop, for instance, L'Oréal recently decided to lure customers with a 20-ml "petite" bottle of one expensive perfume, pricing it at $55, compared with $175 for the traditional 100-ml size. The move gave customers a size they could more easily afford but actually created a 57 percent price hike per milliliter—$2.75/ml versus $1.75/ml. Similarly, many professional baseball teams have lately determined that they can maintain attendance even at high ticket prices if they make game day more affordable by lowering prices on concessions. Customers are less likely to feel outraged by an expensive ticket than by a hot dog that costs twice as much as one bought outside the ballpark. Moreover, lowering the concession prices on known value items that are easier to compare helps everyone feel they received good value at the game.

Large companies with thousands of products face a significant challenge in pricing appropriately for a downturn. But it's often possible to apply new pricing rules to categories of products. One European manufacturer of construction-related products, for example, had tens of thousands of SKUs. To simplify pricing, it grouped the products into three "buckets." Bucket #1 included products that were highly differentiated and that customers valued highly. Bucket #3 included commodity-like products over which the manufacturer had little pricing power. In the middle was Bucket #2. The company applied cost-plus pricing rules to each bucket, but the "plus" was higher for the buckets with more differentiated or more highly valued products. To gather the necessary data, the company relied partly on internal statistics and partly on its managers, who gathered at workshops to run through lists of products, quickly putting them into one bucket or another. This approach to variable product pricing helped the manufacturer raise its earnings roughly 20 percent.

Strategy: Short-term Survival, Long-term Success

A company's options during an acute downturn are determined by its strategic and financial position, as we have observed throughout this book. A small number of businesses occupy strong positions on both of these dimensions and have truly differentiated products or services, which enables them to maintain price levels.

Even then, these companies work hard to deliver higher value for the same price. That can be as costly as cutting prices in the short term, but it preserves pricing integrity for the long term. When Amazon launched the Kindle at $399 in November 2007 (just before the start of the recession), many analysts thought customers would balk at the price, especially since the Sony Reader was available for $100 less. Instead, the Kindle sold out. The Kindle 2, launched in February 2009 at $359, continues to exceed sales expectations at this writing.

While most companies cannot easily hold the line on prices this way, it's a mistake to lower prices without considering the strategic implications. Ask yourself: Where should our prices be in three years? How will short-term actions help us or hurt us on the way to that objective? Aggressive, highly visible discounting, for instance, may cheapen a brand in customers' minds. It may persuade customers that they paid inflated prices in the past and should now take their business elsewhere. Slashing prices also makes it hard to raise prices when conditions improve. Saks Fifth Avenue, as we noted in an earlier chapter, actually hurt its position in the luxury-goods market by sharply reducing prices in the 2001 recession; its earnings were slower to recover than those of competitors. It may have worsened its situation once again through deep price cuts in 2008.

Making the right strategic decisions about pricing can often amount to a chess match. You must consider the whole board and plan several moves in advance. Understanding the market positions of competitors and profit pools in the industry is crucial. But a static view of competitors doesn't help; you need to anticipate their future actions based on their share of key segments, relative cost position, capacity utilization, and financial health. Your industry structure also plays a key role in determining the pricing strategy that will ultimately maximize your profits. What can you do that your competitors will be unwilling or unable to copy? As we noted earlier, markets are not monolithic, and there will be pockets of opportunity created by high share in one segment or low-cost position in another that allow companies to target the most effective pricing moves. At the same time, companies must be careful not to destroy the profit pool in their industry.

Consider the case of a company operating in an industry with high fixed costs and weak competitors. By cutting prices too much it might risk initiating a price war that is destructive for everyone. One large real estate owner, for example, determined that, while it certainly didn't want to lose share in a down market, it also didn't want to gain more than a point or two. Why? Because any scenario in which it gained significant share in the face of falling overall demand would drive competitors to lower prices so much that its own lease rates and profits would plummet.

Build Muscle Now—You'll Need It Later

Throughout this book we have emphasized the critical importance of continuing to invest in your business during the downturn. When it comes to pricing, investing means spending the time and resources required to build real pricing muscle—the capabilities you will need both to survive the current turbulence and to emerge stronger and better able to compete once the economic environment improves. If it hasn't happened already, someone in your industry is likely to go to market with a game-changing pricing strategy. Your ability to react quickly and skillfully will determine much of your business performance over the next twelve to twenty-four months.

The need is clear: despite the powerful link between better price realization and bottom-line performance, pricing is often an underdeveloped function. Most companies have few, if any, dedicated pricing professionals. Individuals who do focus on pricing tend to lack the analytical skills necessary to fully grapple with its complexities, and they rarely command the respect of the broader organization. The good news is that there has never been a better time to build your bench with skilled professionals.

Whatever your talent pool, however, you can get to work on pricing right now. The key is to focus on the three levels: tactical moves, product pricing, and the strategic overview. Better pricing helps companies stabilize their business in a downturn and build profits in the future.

Pursue Game-changing Acquisitions and Partnerships

For many executives, doing a deal in a downturn seems risky and impractical. Credit markets aren't functioning normally, so financing is expensive and hard to come by. Cash reserves need to be guarded as a safety net in case the economy stays bad. Equity markets are depressed, so acquirers and targets alike are wary of stock-based transactions. A major deal could distract management from strengthening the core business and bring unforeseen hazards.

Acquisitions are certainly more challenging in a downturn. The number and value of deals tend to drop dramatically during and immediately after a recession. The aggregate value of deals in 2002, for instance, right after the 2001 recession, came to only about $1.2 trillion. That was less than half the aggregate deal value four years earlier and about one-third of the value four years later. Government-brokered mergers aside, the current recession may end up provoking an even more dramatic drop in deal value.

These constraints make it impossible or imprudent for some companies to enter the deal market. But for companies that are relatively strong strategically and financially, recessions present rare opportunities to improve their competitive position through acquisitions and partnerships. According to our analysis of more than twenty-four thousand transactions between 1996 and 2006, acquisitions completed during and right after the last recession (2001–2002) generated almost triple the excess returns of acquisitions made during the preceding boom. ("Excess returns" is defined as shareholder returns from four weeks before to four weeks after the deal, compared to peers.) This finding held true regardless of industry or the size of the deal. Overall, research shows, companies that acquire in bad times as well as in good outperform boom-time buyers over the long run. General Dynamics, Johnson & Johnson, and JPMorgan Chase have all built strong competitive positions by buying throughout the business cycle.

So what kind of approach makes sense? The most important objective of mergers and acquisitions in any economic environment is to help execute a company's strategy. In a downturn that strategy will almost certainly focus on strengthening the core business. No company can hope to weather the downturn without a strong core, and M&A can be a valuable tool for reinforcing it. In a recession, M&A serves another purpose as well: creating strategic options. The post-recession landscape, after all, is going to look very different from the one we have been operating in for the past twenty years. No one really knows, for instance, how supply chains may be forced to change, what the financial system will look like, or whether consumers have changed their spending patterns for a generation to come. As companies ride out the storm, they need to position themselves to emerge from the downturn both as strong and as flexible as possible.

Some have the resources to expand their strategic options through acquisitions, in spite of the obstacles presented by the downturn. Pfizer's agreement to acquire Wyeth, for example, buys some time for Pfizer as the patents expire on several of its leading medicines. Other industries are likely to consolidate as market leaders attempt to increase their options by expanding in scale or scope—wireless phone companies, for example, adding content and software capabilities. The equity market isn't necessarily an obstacle to stock-based deals in any of these cases, since both the acquirer's and the target's shares are likely to be equally depressed.

Partnerships, joint ventures, and strategic alliances will be a more likely course for many companies to create the right options, given the risks and financing constraints on deal making in a downturn. Alliances give companies the opportunity to compete under a number of different scenarios without the inflexibility or expense of an acquisition. The 2008 deal between Morgan Stanley and Smith Barney, for example, was structured as a joint venture rather than a merger. Nokia established a joint venture in early 2009 with the Indian company HCL Infosystems to offer services such as navigation and music for mobile phones. These kinds of partnerships become more common during downturns and can lead to mergers or acquisitions down the road.

Of course, acquisitions can be disastrous in a downturn if companies go about them the wrong way. One key to avoiding traps is having a clear strategy. A company with a well-thought-out strategy for taking advantage of the changing environment is likely to avoid being drawn into poorly considered acquisitions. Instead, M&A becomes a tool for executing its strategy. That requires an investment thesis tailored to its strategic priorities, the right list of targets, and a well-prepared team ready to act quickly when the time is right.

Investment Thesis: Strengthening Your Base of Competition

The vital discipline for strategic M&A in any economic environment is the investment thesis—a statement that articulates why buying an asset or business will make your existing business more valuable. Broadly speaking, companies create and sustain strategic advantage through some combination of five factors: cost position, brand strength, customer loyalty, ownership of a distinctive set of assets, and government protection. Procter & Gamble, for example, is built mainly on brand power and customer loyalty; the cable company Comcast is built primarily on asset ownership (local cable networks) and government protection (local rules granting it monopoly status). Advantages in any area constitute a company's basis of competition. Understanding that basis of competition—and how a proposed transaction will strengthen it—is the starting point for any successful deal.

Companies fail to understand the importance of an investment thesis even in good times—one reason that so many deals lead to buyers' (and shareholders') remorse. A few years ago, Bain surveyed two hundred fifty senior executives who had been involved in sizable acquisitions. More than 40 percent admitted they had *no* investment or strategic thesis behind their transactions. But when companies make deals that do strengthen their basis of competition—in good times or bad—they increase their long-term earnings potential. In one survey of acquirers involved in both successful and unsuccessful deals, for instance, we found that about 80 percent of successful transactions were based on a clear investment thesis. For failed deals, the proportion was only about 40 percent.

In a downturn, deals are riskier and harder to pull off, which makes it all the more important that each transaction strengthen a company's basis of competition. Verizon Wireless, for instance, has spent millions to strengthen its brand in the minds of consumers: virtually everyone in the United States has seen the ads asking, "Can you hear me now?" and touting the "power of the network." But in wireless telecommunications, a brand's strength depends not just on name recognition and warm feelings on the part of consumers; it depends on state-of-the-art technology and continually expanding geographic coverage.

Those imperatives don't change whether the economy is booming or slumping. That's why Verizon Wireless has kept up a steady stream of acquisitions designed to bolster its brand on these fronts, including forty deals during the period from 2004 to 2007. And that's why it has continued on the acquisition trail even in the downturn, closing a deal to buy Alltel for $28.1 billion in January 2009. The Alltel acquisition gives Verizon Wireless access to additional territories, including fifty-seven rural markets that the company does not yet serve. Verizon Corp., majority owner of

Verizon Wireless, reported a 16.4 percent increase in earnings for 2008 compared to 2007. That increase is fueled by continuing growth in the wireless unit, which in turn has been fed by the unit's focus on using acquisitions to build brand strength.

For Lafarge, the world's largest cement company, the purchase of Egypt's OCI Cement Group, a unit of Orascom Construction Industries, in December 2007 was intended primarily to reinforce its cost position. Lafarge's long-term strategy is to increase its presence in emerging markets; to do so, it needs to stay price competitive. By buying OCI Cement, Lafarge acquired a well-regarded firm in a region where there are massive building projects going on—all of which, of course, require cement. It also gained additional scale, which should help it keep costs and prices low.

What's unusual is that the shares of the acquirer rose markedly (11 percent) after news of the deal broke. Though Lafarge's stock has since been battered by the general slump, its operating income rose more than 50 percent in the first half of 2008. Margins also increased. Most of the credit for that performance goes to the company's emerging markets operations, which accounted for about two-thirds of earnings. The deal has yet to be tested over time, but Lafarge appears better positioned than before to handle the current conditions.

Danaher Corporation has built its acquisition strategy around the investment thesis of strengthening its base of real assets. Danaher owns a large number of highly specialized, niche-oriented manufacturing businesses and operates them according to a distinctive philosophy and set of processes known as the Danaher Business System. It has maintained a rapid pace of acquisitions through good times and bad, and has been largely successful at incorporating the newly acquired companies into its business model. During the last downturn, for instance, it made ten significant acquisitions, including buying Marconi Commerce Systems, now known as Gilbarco Veeder-Root. Gilbarco is a leading global supplier of fuel-dispensing equipment; it recently introduced a dispenser with a live Internet connection, allowing motorists to view Google maps, search Google's local business listings, and then print out directions. Gilbarco was part of Danaher's third-most profitable product line in 2008. This 2001 acquisition contributed to its parent's stellar performance during the subsequent recovery, in which Danaher's shares outperformed the S&P index by a factor of three.

Preparation Leads to Success

Too often, an acquisition begins when an investment banker calls the CEO with a potential target and a deal book. Corporate development staffers quickly give the book a cursory review and do a superficial industry overview. If the deal looks interesting, they construct a valuation model and conduct financial and legal due diligence.

But this approach delivers mixed results at best. If an acquisition team is reacting rather than acting, it's likely to pursue deals with prices below the valuation model, deals with limited upside and almost unlimited downside, and deals whose numbers can be massaged until they meet corporate hurdle rates. The team will turn down transactions that appear to be too expensive but actually are not in terms of their long-term strategic benefits. And it will fail to uncover opportunities it might have turned up on its own if it had followed a strategic road map.

In contrast, seasoned deal makers such as Cintas, the uniform manufacturer, know their basis of competition and are always thinking about the kinds of deals they should be pursuing. Their corporate M&A teams work with individuals who are closer to the ground in the line organizations to create a pipeline of priority targets, each with a customized investment thesis. They systematically cultivate a relationship with each target so that they are positioned to get to the table as soon as (or even better, before) the "For Sale" sign goes up. By this stage, savvy acquirers are likely to have months or even years invested in the prospective deal. As a result, they're often willing to pay a premium or act more quickly than rivals because they know what they can expect to achieve through the acquisition. Acquisitions on this basis helped Cintas sustain its sales growth for thirty-nine consecutive years.

In a deep downturn, resources are scarce and the cost of a wrong move may devastate the acquirer. To go into a deal without this kind of preparation is like jumping into a lake blindfolded—you don't know whether there's a rock right under the surface. Of course, a steep downturn can also present sudden buying opportunities to a well-prepared acquirer, as we noted earlier. In February 2008, JPMorgan Chase had told investors it needed investment-banking capabilities, like those of Bear Stearns, to meet its growth goals. In May, Bear Stearns suddenly became available in a government-brokered deal. Because JPMorgan already knew exactly what it needed, it was quickly able to commit to acquiring an incremental $1 billion in earnings capacity, even after meeting shareholder demands to raise the price once the initial deal was signed.

Getting the Deal Done

Turbulence brings deal-making opportunities, but the obstacles presented by a downturn can stall even a well-prepared company. Focusing on three practices can help guide companies to get deals done.

First, ratchet up the level of diligence you expect from your M&A team. Some of the deals on Wall Street, for example, have turned out to be less attractive than the acquirers initially believed and may cost the acquiring CEOs their jobs. Corporate buyers seeking targets in the same industry are particularly likely to fall into the trap of inadequate diligence because executives believe they know the industry. They often conduct a quick and sometimes cursory regulatory review while failing to ask the big strategic questions—and then they are unpleasantly surprised when the target turns out to be more liability than asset. Private-equity buyers, by contrast, rarely make that mistake: they know what they don't know and so are careful to uncover any hidden traps.

Second, tailor your list of targets to the new valuations. Many companies are relatively cheap in a downturn because their shares are trading at low levels. But some companies are cheap for good reason, and the adage that you get what you pay for applies to deals as much as it does to anything else. It is possible to strengthen your company's core business or create new strategic options at a reasonable price. A target that has seen its stock decline, for instance, may quickly agree to be acquired by a stronger company whose stock has also declined. It seems like a fair exchange of assets rather than a predatory raid, and it is more likely to lead to synergies in the future. This is why the most common near-term deals are likely to be consolidations or other intra-industry transactions.

Third, update the target list to reflect the changing environment. The business climate in the future is likely to be less freewheeling, more tightly regulated, less leveraged, and more risk averse. Some of the large banks that recently acquired mortgage companies or investment houses may never be able to return those businesses to their previous levels of growth and profitability, simply because the environment in those industries is likely to be so different. There are plenty of other unanswered questions about the future as well. Once-successful business models may no longer work. Onetime market leaders may be permanently compromised. Yet you may want to add businesses to your list that you think are likely to thrive in a different environment. A clear investment thesis reflecting the new reality is more important than ever.

Can a company's portfolio actually emerge stronger from the kind of economic hurricane we're seeing right now? In many cases, yes, as long as the deals the company makes are based on sound assessment of the new conditions. Don't assume that things will return to "normal." Don't assume that conventional mergers and acquisitions are your only options; the scarcity of capital is likely to make joint ventures and alliances increasingly popular. Above all, don't use deals to re-shape your company's competitive foundation. Use them instead to strengthen it, to do what you do better. Acting on these principles is the first step toward M&A success, in turbulence as well as in calm weather.

Conclusion

Putting It to Work

Turbulence creates extraordinary threats and opportunities. Unlike "normal" times, when leaders can win through raw power by simply staying the course, turbulence calls for strategic finesse. It demands rapid, sometimes radical responses to conditions that were unimaginable just a few months before. It requires innovative approaches to strategic positioning, organization design, cost reduction, cash management, customer loyalty, pricing, acquisitions, and more—at a time when heavy stress on the business makes innovation most challenging.

The insights and tools we have covered in this book are making a difference for companies right now. But even the most powerful ideas depend on people to put them to work. For executives willing to act, turbulence creates a passing zone, and not just during the bumpy ride down when the economy is contracting and competitors are getting knocked off course. As the economy improves, well-prepared companies can take advantage of the opening. They can accelerate hard and secure leadership positions.

As we have argued in the previous chapters, however, actions must be well-informed to be effective. They need to be tailored to an objective assessment of a company's individual strengths and weaknesses—based on where they stand *today*, not yesterday. Many industry leaders stumble during recessions, for example, because they assume that a strong market position is always an insurance policy against trouble. Sometimes their executives postpone taking precautions. Other times they reach for the same levers they pulled in the past, such as hedging their bets by diversifying. When business worsens anyway, they often overreact. They slash costs and staff indiscriminately, cut capital expenditures, squeeze suppliers, and avoid strategic acquisitions.

The better approach is slow-in, fast-out, like a good driver heading into a sharp curve. Winners in turbulence brake quickly heading into a downturn by managing costs carefully and consistently. As the downturn intensifies they focus on what the company does best, reinforcing the core business and spending judiciously to gain share. They aggressively monitor the competition to ensure they have the best possible line through the curve. They take better care of their most valuable customers, simplify and strengthen their organization, and look for unusual opportunities for strategic acquisitions. All these moves set companies up to accelerate at the apex of the curve, when the economy starts to improve.

As we've said throughout this book, there is no single course or set of prescriptions that works best for every downturn or every company going through a period of turbulence. Survival and growth require focusing on the long term as well as on the short term and adjusting to conditions that can change very quickly. That's one reason that companies with strong cultures of innovation tend to do better in downturns—not because they push out breakthrough products and services (although many do), but because their organizations are geared to rapid adaptation. They are constantly looking for the bumps and curves ahead and figuring out how they can navigate most effectively through them.

The recession that began in 2007 is one of the harshest in recent memory and one of the longest as well. But companies that take the kind of actions we recommend in this book can get through the downturn. When the recovery finally comes—and it will—they will be ready.

Notes

1. A recession is usually defined in the press as two consecutive quarters of decline in real gross domestic product. The actual definition used by the National Bureau of Economic Research (NBER) the Cambridge, Mass–based organization that determines the beginning and end of recessions, is both more comprehensive and more complex. That needn't concern us here, except to note that the NBER typically announces the beginning or end of a recession many months after the relevant date has passed.

About the Contributors

James Allen ("Clarify Strategy: Choose Where and How to Win") is a Bain partner in London and co-leader of the firm's Strategy practice.

Rob Markey ("Protect and Grow Customer Loyalty") is a Bain partner in New York and leader of the firm's Customer Strategy and Marketing practice.

Marcia Blenko ("Strengthen the Organization") is a Bain partner in Boston and leader of Bain's Organization practice.

Mark Gottfredson ("Manage Complexity to Drive Performance Improvement") is a Bain partner in Dallas and leads the firm's Performance Improvement practice.

Hernan Saenz ("Streamline G&A") is managing partner in Bain's Dallas and Mexico City offices and a senior member of the firm's North American Performance Improvement practice.

David Sweig ("Tightly Manage Cash Flows and Liquidity") is a Bain partner in Chicago and a senior member of Bain's Corporate Renewal Group.

Dianne Ledingham ("Turbocharge Sales") is a Bain partner in Boston and a senior member of the firm's Customer Strategy and Marketing practice.

Ouriel Lancry ("Price for Today and Tomorrow") is a Bain partner in Chicago and a senior member of the firm's Customer Strategy and Marketing practice.

David Harding ("Pursue Game-changing Acquisitions and Partnerships") is a Bain partner in Boston and co-leader of the firm's M&A practice.

Paul Judge (series editor) is editorial director of Bain & Company.

About the Author

Darrell Rigby is a global expert on corporate strategy and innovation. He joined Bain & Company in 1978 and leads the firm's global Retail and Innovation practices. He has worked with the CEOs and senior executives of many major international companies, leading assignments in corporate strategy, innovation, and change management in a wide variety of industrial and consumer industries, including high technology, health care, retail, and financial services.

In 1993, Rigby founded and launched Bain's Management Tools Survey, a global survey on the usage of, satisfaction with, and effectiveness of several widely used management tools among a broad range of senior executives.

Rigby is a frequent speaker and author on strategy issues, including innovation, managing in turbulence, customer strategy, and change management. His articles have appeared regularly in *Harvard Business Review*. He has been a keynote speaker at global business conferences and has appeared on CNN Moneyline, NBC, CNBC, and Bloomberg.

Prior to joining Bain, Rigby earned an MBA from Harvard Business School with high distinction (Baker Scholar). He is a graduate of Brigham Young University, where he received a BS in business management summa cum laude.